COMPLETE GUIDE TO FISHING

Trolling

COMPLETE GUIDE TO FISHING

Trolling

MASON CREST PUBLISHERS, INC.

COMPLETE GUIDE TO FISHING – **Trolling** has been originated, produced and designed by AB Nordbok, Gothenburg, Sweden.

Publisher
Gunnar Stenmar

Editorial chief
Anders Walberg

Design, setting & photowork:
Reproman AB, Gothenburg, Sweden

Translator:
Jon van Leuven

Nordbok would like to express sincere thanks to all persons and companies who have contributed in different ways to the production of this book.

World copyright © 2002
Nordbok International,
P.O.Box 7095,
SE-402 32 Gothenburg, Sweden.

Published in the United States by
Mason Crest Publishers, Inc.
370 Reed Road, Broomall, PA 19008
(866) MCP-BOOK (toll free)
www.masoncrest.com

First printing
1 2 3 4 5 6 7 8 9 10
Library of Congress Cataloging-in-Publication Data on file at the Library of Congress

ISBN 1-59084-496-3

Printed and bound in Jordan 2002

Contents

 Preface

One can easily get the mistaken impression that trolling has to do only with equipment, boats, electronics and a vast range of accessories. Certainly it is a "gear-intensive" kind of fishing, but it is far more than that. Drag-fishing from a boat offers infinite opportunities to challenge big fish with relatively light equipment. Thanks to downriggers, for instance, we can present lures at enormous depths on sensitive rods, and with much thinner lines than the conditions would otherwise demand.

It is therefore not difficult to argue against those who consider trolling an unsports-manlike way of fishing. If other methods are to be compared, trolling is as sporting as any of them. Indeed, many former salmon flyfishermen are willing to exchange their fly rods for trolling rods. We might even find a greater sporting value in the use of trolling equipment to attract a strike from a fat, silvery salmon or trout as it hunts in a sea or lake, than in trying again and again with a fly to provoke the same fish while it lingers, brown and emaciated, over a spawning site in a river.

Regardless of which waters you choose to wet your line in, trolling makes it possible to exert your own control over the fishing to an unprecedented extent. On the other hand, whether you fish from a cheap little car-roof boat or a fully outfitted "fishing machine", a strong feeling of freedom and independence is conveyed by seeking the fish in an apparently unfathomable mass of water. Sometimes it may be like looking for a needle in a haystack, but you can take comfort in knowing that 90% of the fish are usually located in just 10% of the water. And the capacity to find and challenge the fish in this limited region is precisely what distinguishes the seasoned, successful troller from the newcomer.

Trolling through the Ages

Among sportfishermen, trolling has always involved the use of a moving boat with sportfishing equipment – in other words with a rod, reel, line, and lure or bait. It is thereby distinguished from methods of dragging for fish which do not directly fight them with a rod and reel.

Certainly trolling is the most international of all sportfishing techniques. It is an approach that can be either simple or advanced, and can be applied to small fish as well as to giants weighing hundreds of pounds. Moreover, it is a method that, with modern accessories, enables one to cover large areas of water and, on a very sporting basis, to make contact with the fish almost regardless of where they occur in a river, lake or sea.

To a growing extent, trolling is concentrated in large water bodies, often with deep and flowing waters, where the majority of fish are not accessible by traditional fishing with a casting rod. It is primarily seaworthy boats and modern navigational aids that have paved the path to fishing waters which, previously, were reserved for nets and other massive-catch equipment.

Contacting fish on the wide open spaces of water is an exciting challenge that involves not only skill at sportfishing, but also good knowledge of fishing biology and navigation. The fish one fights in open waters are almost always in excellent condition – fish that take every chance to show what they are worth in terms of strength, endurance and speed.

In most fishing situations, the external circumstances – such as weather, wind, currents, water level and bottom structure – are more important than the fish itself for the dimensioning of equipment. And it is on this key point that the downrigger has revolutionized modern sportfishing. Downrigger enables you to fish with feather-light baits, and catching fish at very great depths.

Trolling can be done by either an individual or a team. It can be an ideal family diversion, where everybody on board is engaged – irrespective of age, gender, or prior experience. Besides, it is amenable to handicapped persons and does not demand an ability to cast or move for long distances under one's own power. In ice-free waters, it can be done around the clock and all year round, unless the fishing regulations say otherwise.

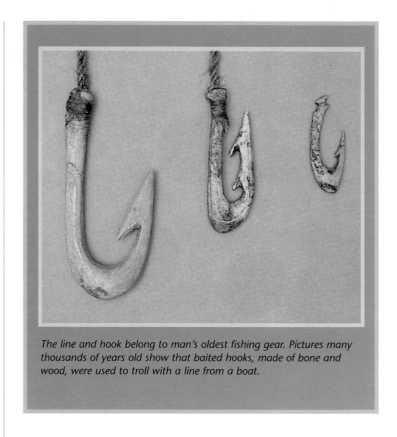

The line and hook belong to man's oldest fishing gear. Pictures many thousands of years old show that baited hooks, made of bone and wood, were used to troll with a line from a boat.

Classic fishing method

Though we have no exact evidence of when the rod made its trolling debut, older fishing literature mentions pioneering trollers in both fresh and salt water, very often where such beautiful, pugnacious, and tasty fish as salmon and tuna live and feed.

A hundred and fifty years ago, the largest lake in Sweden – and in Western Europe – gave rise to what, as far as I know, is the oldest description of lake trolling with a rod. The fishing inspector A. R. Geijer related it as follows:

"When fishing with swivel lures in Vänern, it is best to have four of them out at different depths, in order to determine how deep the salmon are keeping for the day. At the first strike on one or two swivel lures – often two or three are taken at the same time – the rowers should stop the boat instantly, pull in the rear oars, and slowly draw up the swivel lures that have not been striked. But the salmon, or other fish that have striked, can run out with the loose line: usually he runs out quickly for 25-50 meters, and stops. He can then be carefully tired and, finally, boarded with a land-

Waters full of fish in majestic surroundings have attracted many sportfishermen to Scandinavia.
One of the first to thoroughly describe the fishing and its methods was Llewellyn Lloyd, an English enthusiast.
This illustration comes from his book "Scandinavian Adventures" (1853) and represents harling, an effective
and popular way of trolling in the great northern salmon and trout rivers.

ing net or gaff. During the 1850s, this was a highly pleasant and profitable way of fishing, and there were many good days on Vänern when I brought up 12 to 15 beautiful, shining salmon weighing 7-25 pounds (3-10.6 kilograms)."

The traditional Indian fishing waters in the American Northwest became a great center for Pacific salmon trolling early on, with the coastal waters and rivers of British Columbia, Washington and Oregon attracting sportfishermen from near and far. Chinook weighing 83 lbs (38 kg) were taken with rods in these places in the early 1900s.

More than 150 years ago, trolling with a rod, reel and artificial lures, for salmon and trout among other species, was a successful form of leisure fishing in Scandinavian waters. At that time it was often called swivel-lure fishing.

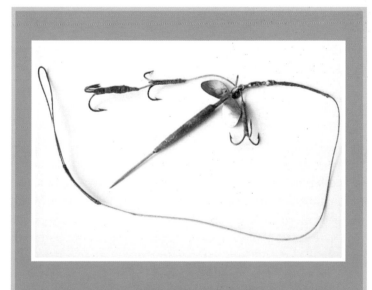

Nineteenth-century tackle for trolling with natural bait. Here, "propeller blades" were used to combine the respective advantages of natural bait and artificial lures for stimulating several of the fish's senses.

Big-game fishing equipment from the first half of our century. The split-cane rod (Salt Water Palakona No.4) as well as the "Fortuna" reel are made by Hardy in England. The line is a 54-strand Cuttyhunk spun from Irish hair. Many big bluefin tuna were vanquished during the 1930s and 1940s in the North Sea and Öresund with this type of gear.

An area as large as the Great Lakes in the northern USA has, of course, attracted many people who can be called pioneering sportfishermen. Still, it is widely accepted that the trolling pioneer George Raff, through his fundamental innovations during the period between the World Wars, was the one who laid the foundations for sportfishing on the Great Lakes. His catches in the deep northeastern part of Lake Michigan, already in the 1920s, revealed colossal concentrations of lake trout and indicated how to get at them with sportfishing equipment.

The big breakthrough for modern trolling techniques, including downrigger fishing, came about in the backwash of environmental conservation efforts in the North American Great Lakes in the 1960s. Twenty years later the wave reached Sweden, which now has the world's best fishing for land-locked Atlantic salmon in Lake Vänern and Lake Vättern. Add to this the fact that in the Baltic Sea, the world's largest brackish sea, trollers take hundreds of Atlantic salmon weighing 45-60 lb (20-27 kg) every year.

The role of big-game fishing

Hunting huge fish in the sea has had tremendous significance for the development of sportfishing, and notably of trolling, around the world. Moreover, it is through big-game fishing that certain places have gained a global reputation and experienced a heyday that would otherwise be impossible.

Tarpon is regarded as the instigator of big-game fishing, and the rivers and coastal waters of Florida were the source of inspiration in the 1880s.

The origins of big-game fishing itself, however, are generally thought to lie at Santa Catalina Island, California. There in 1898, Charles F. Holder, caught a bluefin tuna of 183 lbs (83 kg) and founded the Tuna Club, the world's first big-game fishing club. This organization and its members left a strong mark on the sport during the first decade of our century.

In 1912 and 1913, the trio of William Boschen, Julius vom Hofe and Joe Coxe constructed the first geared reel with a spool that could be disengaged, as well as a drag system that included a reverse catch on the crank. The drag could be externally adjusted via a star wheel. Boschen, a Catalina member, was the brain behind the whole concept, Coxe the source of the idea for the star wheel, and vom Hofe the one who manufactured the prototype reel. To honor Boschen for his pioneering ideas, vom Hofe named the reel B-Ocean.

Fifteen years further on, Oliver C. Grinnell introduced one of the leading lures of all time for trolling: the Japanese feather jig.

West Atlantic and Nova Scotia rod catches came into hot spotlight in 1924, when Zane Grey, the great trolling pioneer of saltwater fishing, brought in a tuna of 758 lbs (345 kg). Zane Grey's distinction as a big-game fisherman had an enormous impact on and world-wide significance for sportfishing during period between the World Wars. Grey made pioneering expeditions with his own boats, on the world's seas.

In Grey's wake , such big-game fisherman as Harlan Major, Michael Lerner, Tommy Gifford, S. Kip Farrington Jr., Jimmy Whittall, Lee Wulff, Van Campen Heilner, Philip Wylie and Ernest Hemingway – another writer, whose work gave the sport a great lift appeared on the east coast of North America New fishing arenas, competitions attracting big audiences, and ever heavier fish were the result.

Lerner and Farrington made remarkable catches in Soldiers Rip, Wedgeport, Nova Scotia, which Farrington called "the biggest little fishing hole in the world". The most effective fishing method was no longer angling but trolling at about 4

The downrigger has revolutionized trolling techniques in the last few decades. My first downrigger, made of brass, was built at home during the early 1970s, from a model advertised in an American sportfishing magazine. Equipped with both a line counter and brake, it opened up a whole new world of fishing to me.

The IGFA is an international sportfishing organization, represented in some 75 countries, which registers world records for different line classes and fish species, and supports the worldwide development of sportfishing and fish management.

knots with the hook concealed in mackerel that was dragged about 25 yards (25 m) behind the boat, sometimes with an outrigger pole.

Kip Farrington wrote in *Field & Stream* in 1949 that Öresund – the sound between Sweden and Denmark - was one of the world's best arenas for tuna, that nowhere else on earth was it possible for individual fishermen to take so many tuna on the same day. Swedes and Danes took great numbers of fish over 650 lbs (300 kg), and the record example of 820 lbs (372 kg) rose in 1950 to a Dane, Knud Kyvsgaard. Given the limited resources of the boats in Öresund – most of the fishing was done from cutters – most of the tuna were taken while drifting rather than trolling.

Cairns in northeastern Australia, with the eormous Great Barrier Reef beyond it, is a place that has had enormous significance for the development of saltwater trolling during the second half of the twentieth century. About 60% of all black marlin over 1000 lbs (455 kg) – including a giant of 1442 lbs (635 kg) – have been caught there. The breakthrough came in 1966 when Captain George Bransford, with mate Richard Obach, caught the first 1000-pounder, 1064 lbs (484 kg) to be precise. During high season, there are about 60 highly equipped 50-foot big-game boats operating off "the Marlin Coast".

The pioneering IGFA

It was Michael Lerner of the USA and Clive Firth of Australia who founded the International Game Fish Association (IGFA) in 1939. The organization soon became worldwide, and boasted none other than Ernest Hemingway as vice president from 1940 until his death in 1962. The IGFA began to formulate and print international sportfishing regulations, and to register marine fishing records in accordance with these rules.

The IGFA has been reorganized a couple of times since 1939. At present, one of its main objectives is to promote the best possible protection for species of interest to sportfishermen, and to see that the latter's rights are recognized. A second, and very important, goal is to support programs for tagging sportfish, as well as other scientific efforts to collect data.

Technique and Strategy

A trolling fisherman is like a decathlon athlete. The more fields he masters and combines, the greater his chances of success, whatever the event. Ever more sportfishermen regard trolling as the truly big challenge. This is not only because all-round skill pays off, but, perhaps above all, because trolling in its modern form is one of the most sporting variants of sportfishing activities. Trolling can be done in different a number of different ways from a simple drift boat as well as from an exclusive motor cruiser.

Today's trolling equipment has not only erased traditional concepts and distinctions within trolling. It has also revolutionized the sport in a way that has given boatfishing totally new dimensions. Earlier the "weight" of the gear dictated the depth at which one could fish. Now, thanks to downriggers, leaf-thin lures can be used at a depth of 350 feet (about 100 meters) with a rod and reel weighing no more than ordinary flyfishing equipment. Formerly, too, the line had to be weighted with a sinker in front of the lure, to get it down to a depth of 35 ft (about 10 m). But there are many plugs shaped to easily reach this depth today.

The boat and the equipment aboard, together with biological facts – the whereabouts of the fish and their behavior in different environments – determine, in large measure, the technique and strategy of trolling in the given fishing waters. The technique may involve a choice between surface and depth trolling, or a combination of both. The strategy may consist of how to fish different areas, such as shorelines, deep holes, and skerries. Your decisions often determine how the equipment should be arranged on board the boat, how fast the boat should be driven, and so on. It is through variation that the senses are stimulated, both on and under the surface of the water.

"Systematic" is also a key word for handling the equipment. Place your gear where it is easy to see and reach - and so that it fishes at different depths and distances from the boat without getting tangled.

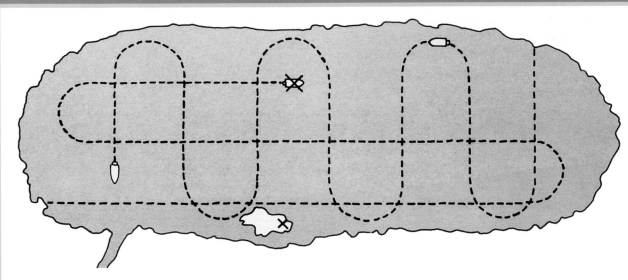

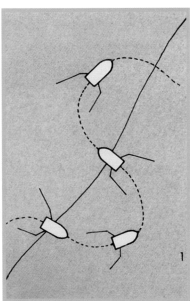

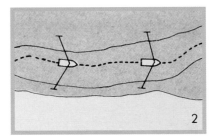

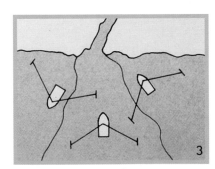

Above: Trolling enables us to fish over large areas and varying depths, as well as often being successful even in unknown waters. The basic fact under all conditions is that the holding places of fish can change in location - depending on the current, depth, temperature, salinity and bottom configuration. Moreover, both prey and predatory fish concentrate at points, banks, rises, inlets or outlets, and underwater springs. To find their real positions, you must systematically comb the water by trolling in parallel lines: for example, first north-south and then east-west. If you lack modern navigation equipment, landmarks and your own floating markers can guide and assist you in fishing out the water efficiently.

1. Instead of trolling in a straight line, follow a zigzag course over a drop-off or rise. When you turn, the innermost lure slows down and, if it is a sinking type, goes deeper. However, a floating type will temporarily approach the surface.

2. A coastal stretch with varying depth contours and temperature zones can be covered effectively with the help of planer boards and outrigger rods, which bring the lures out sideways from the boat.

3. Junctions are often nutritious and diverse in temperature, so they tend to gather fish. Color contrasts on the surface can reveal how the water flows through a tributary's mouth. Cover the fishing area and its zones by moving across it in different directions.

For the initiated sportfisherman, trolling is much more than just aimlessly dragging a lure behind a boat. It is a type of fishing where large areas and varying depths are systematically covered. Guessing can be eliminated by paying attention to the surface features of the water, watching for eddies, temperature spots and birds. With experience, one also learns to understand the language of the water surface under changing conditions, and can quickly analyze questions about the lure or bait, its depth, and the dragging length of the fishing line.

Whether he is surface trolling or depth trolling, and no matter how many rods he is using, it is important for the fisherman to know what effect the maneuvering of the boat has on the lure being trolled. Usually a trolling fisherman zigzags through the water. This makes the lure change speed and run at different depths without the fisherman having to shift gears or speed up the boat. Yawing causes the inside lure to lose speed, going deeper if it is a sinker, or rising if it is a floater. Just as important as knowing how to navigate the boat is knowing which kinds of equipment work well together, and how to present lures and baits in a varied and attractive way in well-thought-out trolling patterns. Using inappropriate equipment can not only lead to problems such as tangles, but also make for inefficient fishing. In other words, the fish may never be attracted to the lure or bait.

Surface trolling

Trolling in surface water is usually done with unweighted line – that is, with only the lure on the end of the line. This can be accomplished with a rod directly from the boat, called flatline fishing, or by guiding the lure away from the boat with the use of an outrigger or a planer board. With the latter, the range of fishing can be broadened and fish can be reached that otherwise might be frightened away by the water turbulence caused by the motion of the boat.

Flatline fishing

Flatline fishing is the oldest and most common variety of trolling. This is what people normally think of as trolling, irrespective of whether it takes place in running water, in a lake, or on the open ocean. The success of flatline fishing usually depends on how far the lure is dragged behind the boat and how it is maneuvered.

For diverse reasons, certain attractive trolling fish congregate periodically over shallow water. If, at that time, there are

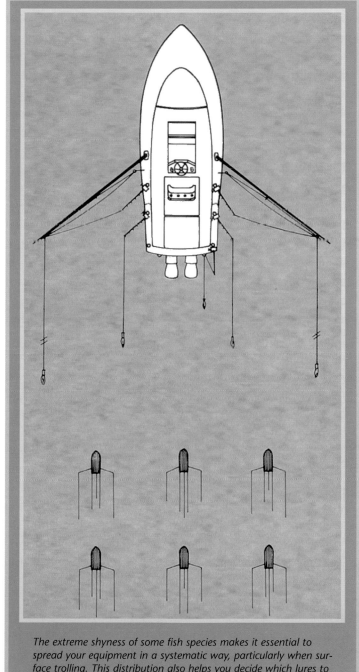

The extreme shyness of some fish species makes it essential to spread your equipment in a systematic way, particularly when surface trolling. This distribution also helps you decide which lures to use and how to manoeuvre the boat. The latter method may go all wrong if you use different types of lines (mono, dacron, wire) in the same trolling pattern, or lures that are too dissimilar.

Normally we describe the trolling pattern as a "W" or "M". The reason is clear from the relationship between the line ends, as illustrated here. To avoid line tangle, the middle line should be either longest or shortest. These standard patterns have been developed through the decades on trolling grounds all over the world.

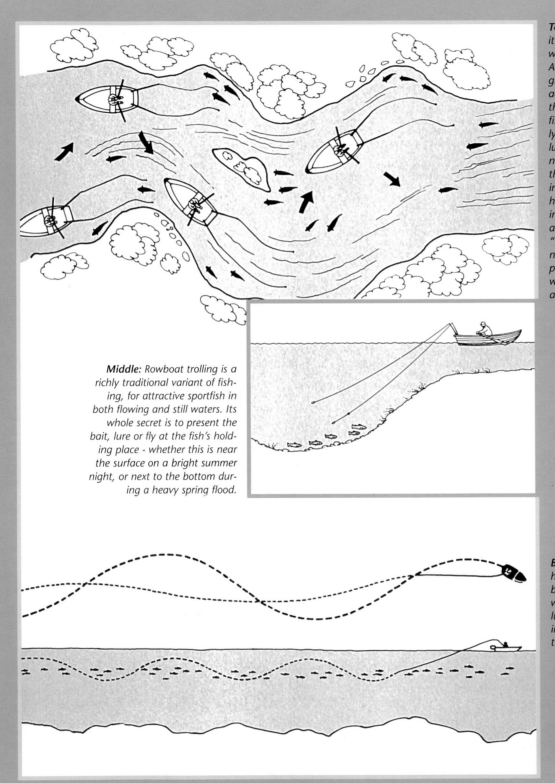

Top: In large, deep salmon rivers it is common to fish by harling, which covers the water effectively. An experienced rower can then give the lure a far more attractive action than what a fisherman on the banks can achieve. The rower/fisherman crosses the river obliquely against the current, while the lures (flies, spoons, wobblers or natural bait) fish downstream over the holding places of fish. By crossing back and forth, he slowly fishes his way downstream. A very important point is that the line and lure, at every turn, should be "stretched out" fully before the next crossing begins. The rowing pace and the setback line length will depend on the river's character and the current strength.

Middle: Rowboat trolling is a richly traditional variant of fishing, for attractive sportfish in both flowing and still waters. Its whole secret is to present the bait, lure or fly at the fish's holding place - whether this is near the surface on a bright summer night, or next to the bottom during a heavy spring flood.

Bottom: A bird's-eye view shows how a lure runs in relation to the boat's zigzag course. The underwater view indicates how the same lure behaves at depth, without increasing the engine turnover or the boat's speed.

several boats at the fishing site, the fish may become especially timid and cautious. If, in addition, the trolling is being done in clear water, the fish can be extremely difficult to entice and the only solution may be to use extra-long fishing lines.

A long line means one that keeps the lure at least 250 ft (75 m) from the boat. This calls for secure hooking, silent lines, and super-sharp hooks. To reduce the wind effect and improve hooking, the flatline may go directly from the tip of the rod to a line release or clip mounted in the boat.

Every year there are, of course, many freshwater, saltwater, and brackwater trollers who claim that they catch lots of fish, such as salmon and salmon trout, almost right up in the foam of the propeller. They maintain that the fish, far from being frightened, are probably attracted by the boat and motor.

In the world of big-game trolling, it is more or less routine to have the lure skip or swim along on the second wave in the wake of the boat. In such cases, a number of different kinds of teasers are normally dragged near the stern.

Simply dragging a long line on a straight course through the water is not very exciting, either for the sportfisherman or for the fish. Variation above and below the surface stimulates the senses. This is where the maneuvering of the boat becomes important. Sometimes an ordinary zigzag is enough to make the lure look like an injured fish.

Ordinarily, however, the zigzag must be complemented by speeding up or slowing down the boat, or else by yawing sharply. When this happens, the zigzag starts to resemble an S-formation. Another good reason for varying the maneuvering of the boat is that fish which escape from the boat, and then quickly return to where they were before, may very well run into the towed lure and strike.

Traditionally, flatline fishing has been classified as surface trolling. Today, however, access to the deep-diving plugs makes this classification seem a bit beside the point. The truth of the matter is that these plugs can go down to depths which, in other circumstances, would be called deep-trolling levels.

Outriggers

The outrigger has its origin in ocean fishing. It was designed to be able to simultaneously position and spread several lures outside the wake of the boat. It therefore projects at a 45-degree angle from the side of the boat. Among big-game fishermen looking for billfish, it is very common to present live bait on an outrigger pole. The bait is presented while skipping on, or swimming just below, the surface. Although the dragging distance from the stern varies, it seldom exceeds 165 ft (50 m).

The number of trolling lures in action behind a boat depends on the size of the craft, the surrounding circumstances – such as waves, wind, currents, and depth of water – and the type of fish one wants to catch. Naturally, even the number of passengers aboard the boat and their competence make a difference.

The size of the boat influences the choice of an outrigger. This determines the size of the lure or bait, which in turn has an effect on the boat speed and line length. An overweighted outrigger offers no attractive lure or bait.

Usually the fisherman employs two outriggers, one to port and one to starboard. Having extra-long outriggers is not as important as how they are used in combination with the navigation of the boat, the fishing tackle and the lure. It is also essential for you to be able to easily and quickly cast an eye at the line release.

The outrigger is equipped with guides or spiders, and usually with a roller guide on top, through which a halyard is passed as on a flagpole. The halyard is provided with a line release, or clip. When the desired amount of fishing line has been rolled from the reel, the line is pinched into the clip. This should be done while the boat is moving slowly. The clipped fishing line is run out toward the tip of the outrigger, where it is placed in position. To prevent it from slipping, the halyard is fastened to the railing with a tensor band. On large and sturdy poles, it is possible to use several halyards and clips at the same time, and thus several lures.

Some fishermen tighten up the fishing line to keep it from getting caught by the wind before the rod and reel are placed in the rod-holder. Others leave a little slack, so that the fish will not feel the resistance right after striking and spit out the lure.

There are also different schools of thought concerning how hard the reel-drag should be set. Some set the drag hard in order to be able to set the hook as soon as the line has been jerked from the clip and stretched. Others use a light drag and let the fish make an initial fast run before the hook is set. However, if the fish jumps, you must strike back immediately.

It often happens that outrigger fish spit out the lure or never get properly hooked. This is because of the slack in the line, called the knockdown, when the line falls as it is jerked from the release by the striking fish. One way to improve on the hooking statistics and catches is to connect a tag-line, sometimes called a stinger-line, to the release or halyard line. The tag-line can be of thick mono (2 millimeters) or dacron (400 lbs) and is usually half a yard (meter) longer than the actual outrigger. It streams aft, typically at a perpendicular angle to the outrigger line when under load. The fishing line will accordingly be dragged farther behind the stern and near the surface than before. When the fish strikes the line is released with less slack and the fish will be better hooked.

Outriggers do not give the same breadth of fishing as one can get when using planer boards. But they are definitely easier to use in combination with downriggers when fishing both widely and deeply. Note that, when using outriggers together with other fishing tackle, the outrigger gear is the first to be deployed and the last to be taken in.

Of course, no rules are without exceptions. The last rule is broken when trolling in Hawaii. There, many boats prefer to use their outrigger poles in a nearly upright position. The pattern used for trolling here is neither to proceed along a broad front, nor to have the lure skip along on the surface. Instead, the idea is to drag the artificial high-speed lures, called kona heads, in a row at 30-130 ft (10-40 m) behind the boat, so that they occasionally break the surface. This causes a trail of bubbles that attracts fish. The technique pays off and results every year in remarkable catches of yellowfin tuna and blue marlin.

Planer boards

The planer board fulfills the same function as the outrigger. It spreads out the lures and makes it possible to fish in water that has not been disturbed by the boat. Fishing with planers is much more common in lakes and coastal waters than on the open ocean. The technique is used primarily during the spring and autumn, when the fish move near the surface or over shallow water. Planers can be used to "serve" lures in water that is too shallow or uncertain for a boat and crew to pass through.

Planer boards come in many models and sizes. When an ordinary planer board is used, the spool or mast must be easy to get at, placed high and as far forward in the boat as possible. This provides a good high line angle between the reel and the planer. It causes the planer to move parallel with, and at approximately the same level as, the boat. The smallest are

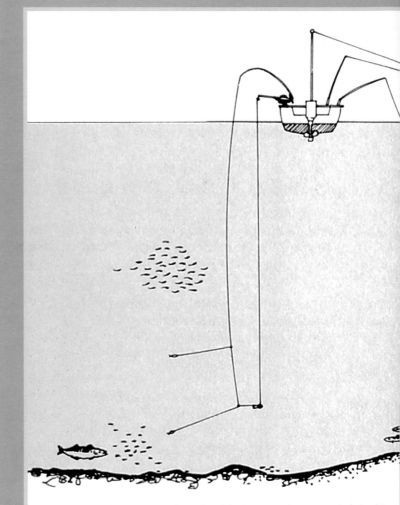

Top: Coastal waters may abound in fish. Some species stay entirely in this zone, though others enter it only periodically. Modern trolling techniques, however, have made it possible to fish these waters even if they are very shallow or sharply plunging.

By using planer boards, you can present lures quite near the shore, for instance where the boat is too deep for the water or where it would frighten the fish. A directional diver will enable you to cover cliff shelves and other formations on a shore slope. A downrigger allows presentation of feather-light lures in, and over, deep edges and holes close inshore.

Bottom: Most fish species migrate between deep and shallow waters. This may happen either seasonally, or several times daily. A point swept by a current, with a deep hole just off it, frequently lies on such a migration route. The illustration shows how to fish a coastal zone and slopes, and finally zigzag around the hole's deep edges.

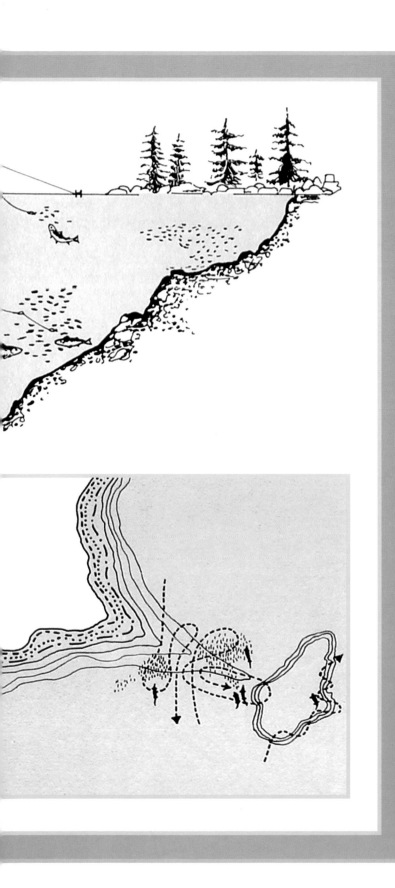

clipped directly to the fishing line. In case of a strike, they are released to slide down the line. They are easy to handle but are also readily disturbed by waves.

How far out the planers are to be placed depends on how many lures or baits you are fishing, how shallow you can go with the boat, and how much space you have in relation to other planer-board fishermen. Some planers allow you to fish up to 250 ft (75 m) from a boat, whereas the smallest have a range of only about 50 ft (15 m).

After the planer board has been put into place, the desired length of fishing line is fed out from the trolling reel. The line is then clipped to a release, which is constructed so as to allow the line to slide along the towline until it reaches the desired position. The rod and reel are placed as far to the stern as possible. When the fish strikes, the line is jerked from the release and the fish is played directly from the rod and reel. The clip slides down toward the plane where it remains hanging, and thus cannot get lost.

Planers may be used to fish surface as well deep-running plugs. The latter demand a little extra resistance from the line release, in order to avoid too many false releases. Do not mix the lures too much, and remember to use lures which work well together – that is to say, which accept the same speed. The length of the dragged fishing line is usually between 15 and 165 ft (5-50 m). Fishing the longest lines nearest the planers reduce the risk for tangled lines.

Depending on the weather, the number of fishermen and their experience, up to half a dozen rods can be deployed from each side of the boat. The disadvantages of planer boards become most apparent during severe weather. They move in a stop-and-go fashion and give false releases. Trying to land a big fighting fish in a heavy head sea causes extra problems because the boat cannot be stopped without risking tangles. If you are alone in the boat when this occurs, there is also a danger that the joy of fishing may become the death of the fisherman.

The tow of the planer is noticeable when steering small boats – especially if only one planer is used, the boat being pulled in its direction. As a matter of principle, when fishing with planers one needs to have plenty of room as one tries to turn the boat. Check to make sure that all planers are moving forward; otherwise the fishing will be inefficient, and you run the risk of tangles or snags.

Deep trolling

A saying that I have heard in many parts of the world is that for every fish you see on the surface, there are ten more in the depths. If so, it is there that you should mainly offer your lures. But how deep is deep, you might ask? No exact answer can be given to this. Over the years, I have learned that what is known as deep trolling in one place may very well be called surface trolling in another.

However, the confusing terminology is not really decisive in trolling. What is important, rather, is that the lures can be presented in a sporting manner at the depths where fish exist, regardless of whether the water is in a shallow flatland lake or a deep ocean trough. And this can now be done – in different ways – much better than in the past.

The line – a crucial factor

How deep a lure can reach on a monoline without extra weight depends upon the diameter and length of the fishing line, the shape of the lure, and the speed of the boat. In a nutshell, one can say that the thinner the line, the more distant the fishing, the better the lure is designed for deep diving, and the slower one trolls, then the deeper the lure will run.

But theory is one thing, and the practice of fishing is another. Here it is not simply a question of getting a lure down to the fish: they also have to be hooked. The longer a monoline, the harder it is to hook the fish. A troller therefore tries to hook the fish with as short a line as possible.

Fast, deep-diving plugs are helpful in this respect. Tests have shown that they can reach to a depth of 33 ft (10 m) using a 12-lb line with a length of 80 ft (25 m). At a speed of

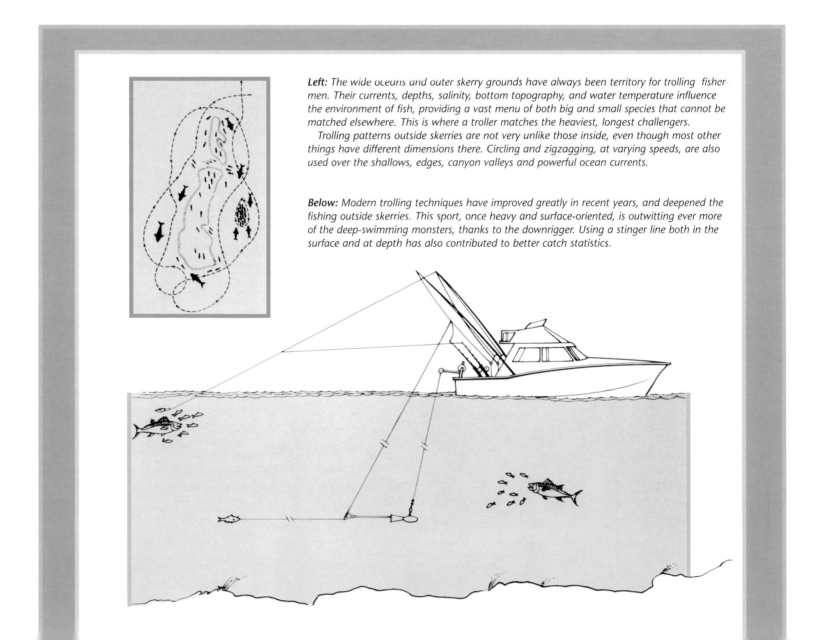

Left: The wide oceans and outer skerry grounds have always been territory for trolling fishermen. Their currents, depths, salinity, bottom topography, and water temperature influence the environment of fish, providing a vast menu of both big and small species that cannot be matched elsewhere. This is where a troller matches the heaviest, longest challengers.

Trolling patterns outside skerries are not very unlike those inside, even though most other things have different dimensions there. Circling and zigzagging, at varying speeds, are also used over the shallows, edges, canyon valleys and powerful ocean currents.

Below: Modern trolling techniques have improved greatly in recent years, and deepened the fishing outside skerries. This sport, once heavy and surface-oriented, is outwitting ever more of the deep-swimming monsters, thanks to the downrigger. Using a stinger line both in the surface and at depth has also contributed to better catch statistics.

1.5 knots, if the lure was released with 165 ft (50 m) of line, the lure descended to a depth of 50 ft (15 m).

An ancient way of reaching thermoclines and bottoms has otherwise been to weigh down the line with some kind of sinker. Today's trollers prefer specially designed sinkers that are shaped so as to give the least possible water resistance and to prevent them from snagging easily. The sinker release type comes in a variety of models, all of which release the sinker when the fish strikes. This revolutionary discovery means that the fish can be played without dragging a heavy weight, thus giving the trolling fisherman a more memorable duel.

Today a troller generally uses mono-, cofilament-, dacron- or superlines – if he or she does not prefer to seek the depths with the help of heavy lines made of lead core or wire. Fishing by these means has a long tradition in many parts of the world, and it has enabled both saltwater and freshwater fishermen to bring up giants from deep currents and bottoms. However, with the arrival of the downrigger in the realm of trolling, the wire line's importance has been diminishing over the past decades.

The advantages are that a feather-light lure can be taken down to great depths with a short line, even in swift currents, and that it is very easy to tell when you have a bite. One needs no special accessories or specially shaped lures to get down to 30 ft (10 m) at 2-3 knots with a line of 100 ft (30 m).

The disadvantages are that the lines often demand special rods and reels, and the fishing must be done with extra care. Nor should they normally be combined with more traditional fishing gear.

The diving planer

Divers have old and global merits in the world of sportfishing. Thanks to various improvements during the 1980s, they are experiencing a well-deserved renaissance, and few trolling fishermen would want them to be missing from the tacklebox. Special high-speed planes are available.

The diving planer is attached to the fishing line above the leader and lure. When the planer hits the water, the resistance of the water causes it to head downward. How deep it goes will depend on its own shape, the lure's shape, the diameter of the fishing line, and the trolling speed. When the fish strikes, the special trip mechanism is released and the fish can be reeled in without much water resistance from the diver.

Some divers can be adjusted so that they move sideways from the boat. These can get down to about 30 ft (10 m) with

Even in a small boat, well-arranged rigging gives good coverage of the water both to the sides and downward.

a 0.45-millimeter line (20 lbs) having a length of 80 ft (25 m). This line diameter is normal for fishing with divers. Even the leader, 3-5 ft (90-150 cm) long, should be at least this thick. All kinds of lures can be fished successfully behind a diver, including dodgers or flashers with squids or flies. The diver itself often seems to function as a lure. The lure is affected by the diver's sensitivity to the movements of the boat, giving it a particularly irrational action.

The diver complements downrigger fishing by widening the parallel pattern of deep trolling. Baits can easily be led over otherwise hard-to-reach shelves on a deep bank. Given a separate line with a special release, it can be used alone as a simple downrigger.

One disadvantage to be reckoned with is that you need a fairly sturdy rod (there are specially designed diving plane rods) when the diver is to be pulled through the water. The pull of the diver on the rod means that the rodholder must also be strong and of high quality. Furthermore – as with other deep-trolling techniques, except that of downrigger fishing – it is difficult to define the depth precisely. The observant fisherman should, however, have no great difficulty navigating through the same trolling patterns as used in surface trolling.

The downrigger

It is said that in the time since sportfisherman started using the outboard motor, no other single piece of equipment has meant so much to fishing as the downrigger. The downrigger has not only deepened fishing but has also widened its horizons.

Generally it can be claimed that, in one way or another, the downrigger plays a role in all sportfishing from a boat, regardless of the type of environment. It provides the fisherman with the ability to determine more precisely how deep or how shallow the lure should run. He is also given the great sporting advantage of being able to adapt his gear to the size of the fish, and not primarily to the surrounding circumstances such as wind, current, and water depth.

A downrigger is a separate piece of equipment that consists of a spool with wire line, and an arm with a guide at the end through which the wire passes. The sinker weight is placed on the end of the wire. The line release is attached to either the sinker or the wire. Most downriggers even come equipped with counters, drag, and rod-holder. The down-

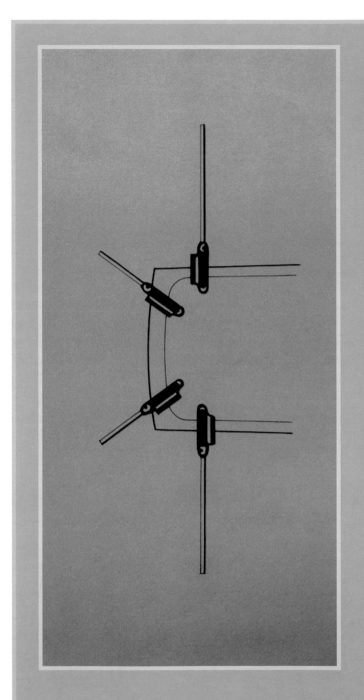

Here the fishing line is mounted in a line release which is coupled to the downrigger's weight. The release can also be placed on the downrigger wire. The line distance between release and lure depends on the fishing depth and the visibility in the water.

The picture shows how you should adapt the number and size of downriggers to the boat's dimensions. It is important to position the rigs so that they will not risk safety on board,

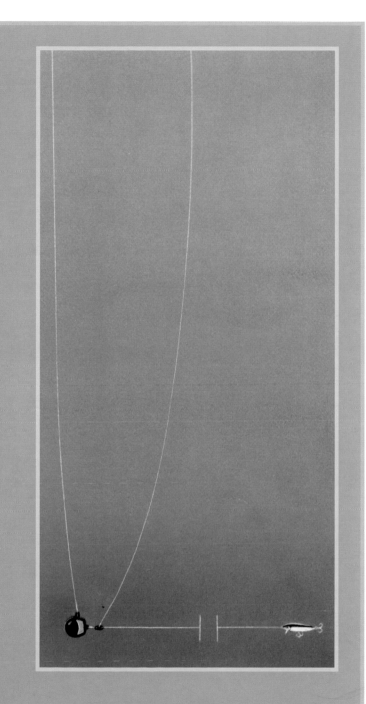

for example by blocking access to a motor. Try also to place them as far astern as possible. But remember that the rod and other items should be easy to reach and keep an eye on.

Long-boomed rigs are best located on the port and starboard decks, and rigs with standard or medium-long booms on the after-deck, since this provides optimum spreading. There are several options for how to mount the rigs in place.

rigger's technical details are described in chapter 3, Trolling Equipment.

The downrigger should be securely mounted, easy to get at, and easy to see. This usually means that it is placed in the stern-most third of the boat. There it can be arranged to point sideways or straight back.

Irrespective of the fishing depth, one should try to keep the sinker as directly vertical under the boat as possible. This is regulated by the sinker's shape and weight. If you can see the sinker in your sonar, then it is in a good position.

The line release is responsible for the first hookup. How hard the release tension should be set depends on type of fish being sought, the trolling speed, and the size of the lure. It is important that the fishing line should not slip in the release. By using several line releases, one can fish several (two or three) lines from the same downrigger cable. This is called " stacking".

The downrigger may be said to function like an outrigger, but in a vertical direction. In some circumstances, it can be used in combinations. Start by pushing the free-spool button on your fishing reel. Use the alarm click and then feed out the desired length of fishing line. This can vary between 3 and 250 ft (1-75 m) depending on the type of fish you are after, how deep they are running, and the depth of visibility. Generally, the deeper you fish, the shorter the line between the release and the lure. A short line allows better hooking, and greater maneuverability of the boat in order to follow irregular bottom contours.

If the fishing reel does not have a line counter, then the dragging length can be estimated, for instance, by eye or by counting the number of hand lengths of line between the reel and the lowest guide on the rod. Place the rod in a rod-holder and the line in the release. Before lowering the sinker weight down to the desired depth, check that the line is not twisted around the tip of the rod.

Remember that the counter indicates how far the sinker is from the point – arm tip or water surface – at which it was set to zero. Therefore, it does not register the level of the sinker and lure with perfect accuracy. Ordinarily a sonar can be used to verify exactly where they are running.

The next step is to reel in the slack and tense the line, so that the specially designed rods assume a J-bend. The line should point as straight down towards the sinker or line release as possible.

A variety of boom lengths on your downriggers will spread out the lures underwater. Models differ as regards the fishing line's attachment and the downrigger's line release, but the line should be fastened so that it cannot slip in the release.

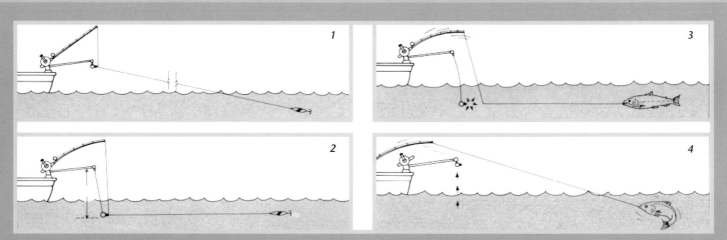

Downrigger fishing involves using light equipment and leaf-thin lures to fish at great depths. The basic technique is shown briefly here.
1. Feed out the line and lure until you reach the desired setback distance. Place the line in the release, which may be on either the sinker or wire.
2. Freespool the reel with your line-out alarm on. Sink the weight and lure to the desired fishing depth, which can be read on the downrigger's counter.

3. When the fish takes, it pulls line free from the release. Usually it is hooked adequately by the release's own resistance at that moment.
4. Grab the rod from the rod-holder, perhaps making an extra strike. Then play the fish directly from the rod. Reel in the downrigger wire and weight as soon as possible.

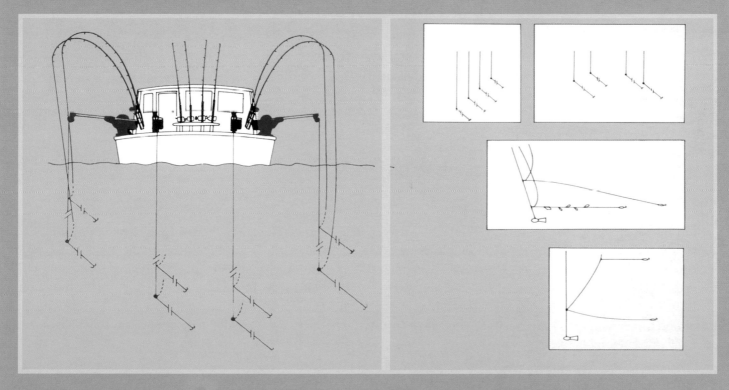

Most downriggers have one or more rod-holders. As shown here, for instance, you can fish with two rods from each downrigger. A reel line is attached in the line release closest to the weight, while a "stacker line" is placed in a release farther up on the wire. It is essential to systematize the rod arrangement on board, so that you can fish well with a minimum risk of line tangle under the surface.

The distance between two line set-ups on the same downrigger wire should be variable, in order to cover a range of depths. Moreover, the setback line distance behind the boat should differ.

Normally the lure is 6-33 ft (2-10 metres) from the weight and line release, but sometimes they are 100-165 ft (30-50 metres) apart. Among other things, the depth of visibility, type of lure, and pattern of currents influence this separation. Generally it is made shorter for fishing deeper.

You can also place several lures close together, to make them look like a school of fish. The same effect is obtainable with diverse models of flashing attractors. By sliding a lure on a short leader along the line, you can give the impression of one fish chasing another. Try to stimulate the fish's aggressivity with your lure arrangement.

Trolling is a fascinating way of fishing. Lining this highroad to the fish are many details for attentive sportsmen to harvest.

Trolling speed

Trolling speed may vary anywhere between a couple of knots and twenty. The range of trolling varieties, however, makes the terminology of speed hard to understand. This is most obvious when, for instance, a marlin troller discusses the subject with a salmon troller. What the former calls slow speed or "no speed at all", the latter takes to be top speed.

The more one trolls, the more one becomes convinced of the great influence the speed of the boat has on the action of the boat as it passes through the water. In the long run, a constant dynamic action has a greater effect than the size, color, and shape of the lure.

There are many factors to consider when the objective is to call forth the lure's most enticing movements. Besides the influence of the boat and the motor, consideration must be given to the current and the presence or absence of wind and waves.

A good estimation of the effectiveness of different kinds of lures under various fishing circumstances is obtained by keeping a fishing log. Remember, though, that if you note a lure as attracting fish "best at 2.5 knots", then this is only valid for the speedometer in your own boat. A speedometer in another boat running parallel to yours may indicate a different figure for the "same" speed. In other words, you cannot easily transfer speed figures from one boat to another.

Each lure has a speed at which it works best. Due to the fact that trollers normally use several lures at the same time, it is important to use lures that are compatible at a given speed. Some lures have a fairly wide range of tolerance with regard to speed. the easiest way to convince yourself of the lure's action is to check it as the lure is let out beside the boat.

As already mentioned, a speed indicator can be a great help. But there may be drastically different temperatures and cur-

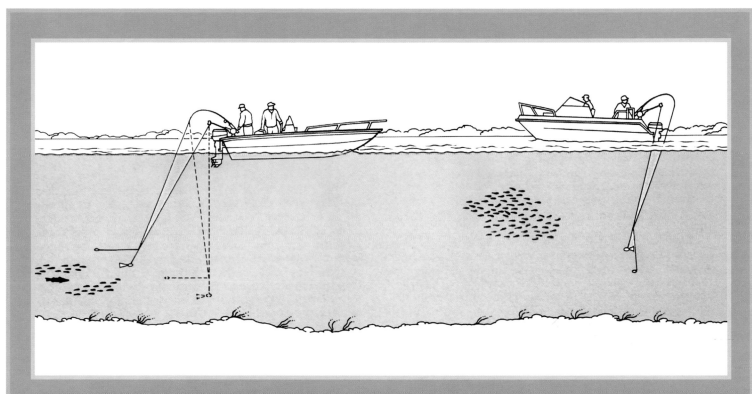

The speed of the boat and lure through the water is decisive for success in fishing. Frequently the conditions at the surface are quite unlike those a few yards below it. For example, currents may be moving in directions opposite to the surface current. The lure will then move very differently from how it did when you tested it at the surface next to the boat.

After a storm, the water mass under a calm surface often flows rapidly in a certain direction. An alert troller can see this from the behavior of his bow waves, from the angles and sounds of his downrigger wires, and possibly from the fact that the fish take only when he is trolling in a particular direction.

Instruments such as a navigator and surface-water speedometer show the speed. If you troll into a current that moves, say, at three knots, the speedometer will show about the same figure. But the navigator, which

detects the average speed over the bottom, might reveal that this is only about half a knot.

In this drawing, the boat at left is trolling forward in a strong current. The downrigger wire and lure are pushed upward and do not fish at the intended depth. But the adjacent broken lines indicate what the ideal conditions would be. The weight is at the "correct" depth and the lure's speed is determined by the boat's. The boat at right is going with the current, at about 3 knots according to its speedometer. Here the sinker and lure do not run attractively, as the current is pushing with almost the same speed. For both situations, a good solution may be to troll broadside to the current, and at different angles to it - as well as to use extremely short or long lead lengths, with lures that vary in shape and weight.

rents at a depth of 100-130 ft (30-40 m) than there are on the surface. As a result, the speed you read on the log at the surface does not always match the speed of the lure in the depths.

How can this phenomenon be detected? The surest way is by using an electronic speed and temperature gauge. This instrument sends information about the water temperature and the speed of the currents in the depths by way of telemetry. See Chapter 4.

If you have learned your lessons about the "best speed" for the lures, then all you have to do is speed up or slow down the boat, be watchful and regularly check the action of the rod tips, and the tension and angle of the downrigger wires.

Temperature can also have a great effect on the speed of the boat and the choice of lure. This is because the reaction time of the fish is, in most cases, dictated by the temperature of the surrounding water. In cool water the fish are more likely to be attracted to a slow lure that is vibrating violently, than to one which passes by quickly looking like a fish. In lukewarm water the desired effect might be the exact opposite. It is definitely the sharp-eyed and quick-witted who reap the harvest in the infinitely fascinating worldwide sport of trolling.

Trolling Equipment

Pulling baits and lures through the water from a moving boat can be done either with a simple hand line, with traditional casting gear, or with specially designed trolling equipment. No other group of sportfishermen enjoys as wide a range of options in this respect as the trolling fisherman does – if he or she wants to be ready for everything from the colorful perch in forest lakes to the powerful giants in oceans.

Trolling equipment is not primarily designed for casting. It can be constructed for trolling with a downrigger, for tolerating the wear of wireline fishing, for making strikes with heavy hooks, for pulling up heavy fish from great depths or for having a large line capacity.

In general, this equipment seems to have a well-established form, but its materials are constantly being developed and improved. Today's trolling fishermen are able, largely because of modern design and new materials with less weight as well as more strength, to adapt their equipment to particular fish species in a more sporting and varied way than ever before.

When choosing the equipment, its balance is important. A good reel, line, rod and lure are adapted well to each other. With compatible gear, and proper maintenance, there will be a minimum of problems and a maximum of fishing time.

Classes of equipment

Different pieces of equipment are usually classified in some way when they leave the manufacturer, so that we can match them together correctly. The most common method of classification is a globally accepted line-class system, developed by the International Game Fish Association (IGFA).

Originally this system was introduced for the registering of world records in several line classes. These are 1 kilogram (2 pound), 2 kg (4 lb), 3 kg (6 lb) 4 kg (8 lb), 6 kg (12 lb), 8 kg (16 lb), 10 kg (20 lb), 15 kg (30 lb), 24 kg (50 lb), 37 kg (80 lb) and 60 kg (130 lb). Each figure gives the highest allowed breaking strength of the line when wet, in order to have a record registered in that class. While the IGFA standards are based on the line's strength, they also include rules for the reel's construction and the rod's dimensions.

Another familiar means of dividing up equipment is to classify it on a scale from ultra light to very heavy, in correspondence with the line's breaking strength. This division,

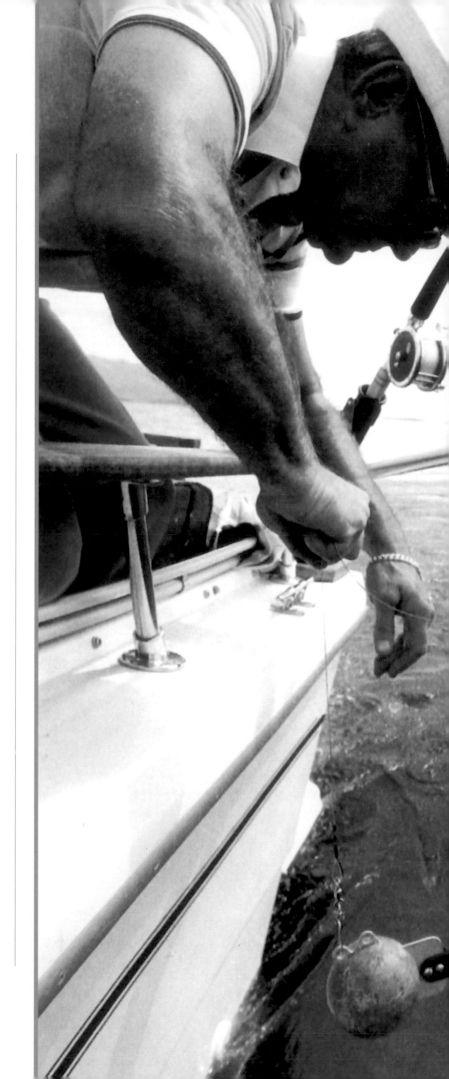

though, is quite flexible. A set-up that proves to be light in a fight with a big tuna will be heavy when it comes to catching ordinary sailfish. Consequently, whether the gear is considered light or heavy depends to a great extent on the fish's size. In any case, the weight classes are: ultralight (1-2 kg), light (4-6 kg), light medium (8-10 kg), medium (15-24 kg), heavy medium (37 kg) and heavy (60 kg). Equipment classified as extra heavy or of "unlimited class" has a line with a breaking strength of more than 60 kg.

There is naturally a vast difference between a set-up in IGFA class 8 kg and one in class 60 kg, as regards strength, weight and appearance. The latter class is built to withstand the real monsters of the world's seas, which sink the scales to at least 500 kg (1,100 lbs) and go by the names of black or blue marlin, bluefin tuna, and the very biggest sharks. By contrast, the former class can be relied upon mainly to tame the leaping salmon of northern latitudes, or the arrow-fast small tuna in southerly waters.

Impacts and rough seas are an aspect of daily life on board, at any rate for the small-boat troller. You should thus insist on a high standard of quality for your equipment from the very beginning, notably for fishing in marine or brackish waters. Of course, you have to do your own part by giving the gear every care and service it requires. This will make your time on board more secure as well as more pleasant. You will also face smaller risks when a dream fish hits the lure, is hooked and jumps up in the air, then bolts away in a long run that almost empties the line from your reel. This is when your relationship with the equipment and with the other members of the crew is revealed.

Regardless of the equipment's line class, it can be used for downrigger fishing. The sinker weight should match the downrigger's size and strength, as well as the type and depth of water.

The rod

Trolling rods differ in their form and materials, depending primarily on how they are used. A deep-trolling rod designed for big salmon and trout in the Baltic Sea has few similarities to a trolling rod for the yellowfin tuna of Hawaii.

The main characteristics of a trolling rod are its length, action and power curve, and the structure and size of its handle, reel seat, and rod rings or rollers. The rod's action shows how it is designed – where the blank flexes, and whether it has fast action, medium action or slow action. In the last case, the rod flexes throughout its length and dampens the fish's movements evenly, whereas tip action means that the rod's upper third is limb and flexes quickly.

The power curve indicates the rod's resistance to deflection. Here the usual division is between light, medium and heavy. With a heavy rod, it is relatively hard to tell how much pressure you are putting on the fish. This factor is most important when you fight fish with soft mouths.

Downrigger rods

A downrigger rod's construction makes it far superior to a conventional rod if it is used in combination with a downrigger. The deeper one fishes, the more obvious this becomes. The chief characteristic of a downrigger rod is the J-shaped action curve, which the rod acquires if it stands up tensed in a rod-holder. The rod's extremely fast tip action helps to hook the fish better, while minimizing the line's chance of slipping in the line release. Provided, of course, that the rod is long enough and the downrigger is suitably placed on board.

Downrigger rods come in lengths between 7 and 10 ft (2.1-3.0 m). Most are 8-9 ft (2.4-2.7) long, and divided in two sections. There are models for both multiplier reels and spinning reels. Rods can also have different power curves.

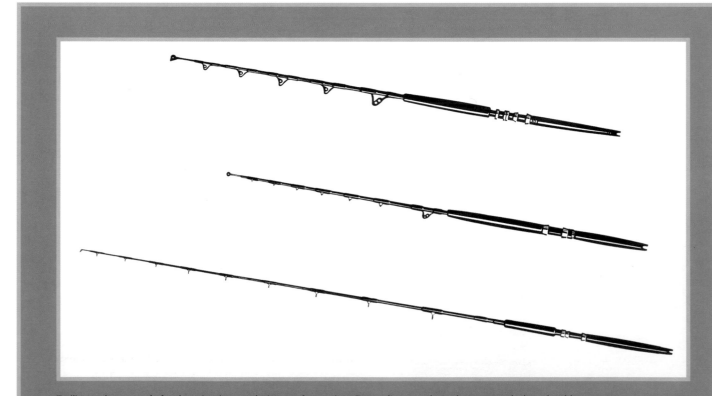

Trolling rods are made for dragging lures or baits, not for casting. Depending on where they are used, they should tolerate standing constantly with strong tension from a downrigger, and being worn by wire lines. They also need enough backbone for powerful strikes with big hooks, and enough capacity to pump up heavy fish from great depths. At top is shown a traditional trolling rod, in the centre a stand-up rod, and at bottom a downrigger rod.

Another striking thing about downrigger rods is their large number of guides, normally from nine to twelve on an 8.5-ft (2.6-m) rod. The guides are closest together at the tip, since they have to lead the line so that it does not lie vibrating against the blank while fishing. This could rapidly ruin even the best line, resulting in lost lures and fish.

The handle should be so long that the rod stands steady in the holder, even on rough seas. A length of 12-14 inches (30-35 cm) will keep the reel and its seat clear of the holder. The foregrip should be at least 5 in (12 cm) long. Both cork and synthetic materials give a good grip, but cork wears down much faster in a rod-holder. The reel seat is another vulnerable part, so the reel seat and its locking ring should be of high quality and keep the reel firmly in place.

The boat's speed, the resistance from the line release when the fish pulls out line, and the rod tip's fast response – all these tend to hook the fish well from the start. A sweeping upward movement when the rod is lifted out of the holder is usually all you need when fishing for salmon. Hard-jawed fish such as pike and walleye demand a stronger counterstrike to get the hook caught.

In recent years, specially designed rods have been introduced for fishing with diving planes. They are normally 9-11 ft (2.7-3.3 m) long, and have a heavy action to be able to pull the plane through the water, 30-50 ft (10-15 m) from the boat. On these rods, too, the guides sit densely in order to control the line.

Stand-up rods

Conventional trolling rods are generally around 7 ft (2.1 m) long, have 5-7 guides including the tip roller, are detachable at the handle, and come with a gimbal butt on the end. The power curve of a classic trolling rod is distributed rather similarly regardless of its class – light, medium or heavy. A weak rod gives fine resistance pressure because of its often evenly distributed action and modest length.

A stand-up rod, in contrast to traditional trolling rods, is primarily built for fighting the fish from a standing position. In European sea fishing, this is the most common fighting position on board. With its action and short length, a stand-up rod is not as ideal for trolling in a rod-holder as the traditional big-game rod, but it is definitely superior for duels along the railing.

The usual length of a stand-up rod is 5-6 ft (1.5-1.8 m). It is not divisible, and the handle is often nearly as long as the blank. Its reel seat sits low, so the reel is easy to balance near your body. The handle's long upper part also enables you to grip it near the center of balance when pulling against the fish. If you play the fish with short, fast pumps, the rod's construction displays all its advantages. To get the most out of these, a fisherman normally uses a very low-hanging rod belt with a gimbal cup, which makes it possible to fight with the hips and legs as well as the arms. A kidney harness can supplement the equipment in the heavier line classes.

Stand-up rods often range over several line classes. For instance, there are rods marked 6-10 kg (12-20 lbs), 15-37 kg (30-80 lbs) and 24-60 kg (50-130 lbs). The short, and frequently tapered, blank may not inspire much confidence, by comparison with traditional big-game fishing rods; but its appearance is deceptive. These rods have a spine which, if properly handled, can lift almost anything up to the surface.

A rod's power curve shows how much it bends under pressure. Its force of resistance is defined as light, medium or heavy. Above is a rod with a stiff blank, and below is one with a soft blank. The action curve, which is often confused with the power curve for a rod, shows where the blank flexes. Here the rod is termed fast, medium or slow.

A downrigger rod under tension. Hallmarks of a trolling rod are its unusual number of guides, and the typical J-bend it assumes when standing tensed in a rod-holder. The many guides are needed to prevent the line from vibrating against the blank, and thus being weakened, while fishing.

The stand-up rod's emergence has enabled contemporary sportsmen all over the world to catch many more fish with three-figure kiloweights from small trolling boats than was possible in the past.

Rod components

A trolling rod consists of the blank, a reel seat, handle and foregrip, ferrules, and guides. The developments in material are very fast, with graphite and mixed materials gaining ground almost everywhere.

The blanks for most contemporary trolling rods are made of composite materials such as graphite and fiberglass, or solely of graphite or tubular fiberglass. In general, graphite rods are more sought-after in the light classes, especially among freshwater fishermen. Carbon-fiber rods feel stiffer than fiberglass rods without loading, but tend to be much more sensitive. A good compromise has been found in the composite rod, which manages to combine the durability of fiberglass with the low weight and sensitivity of carbon fiber.

The handle

Conventional big-game rods are usually detachable at the reel seat, whose main job is to hold the reel steady in a shaky environment. Big-game rods normally have two locking rings that fasten the reel. Reel seats are made of graphite, aluminum, chromed brass, or stainless steel.

The handle may consist of metal, wood, fiberglass, graphite or PVC. A wooden handle can be beautiful, but it requires a lot more maintenance than metal and space-age materials do. Exclusive rods tend to use aluminum, which is lightest but still strong and durable. Some rods in the heavier classes have a curved handle, making it easier to fight from a chair. The rod can be angled more horizontally, with better lever action.

To a growing extent, there is a gimbal nock in the rod's end, even if it is a light one. But you should check that its slot is deep enough, not just decorative. The slot has to make the rod stand more steadily in a holder on the railing, and keep it from turning around during the fight when it is placed in a rod belt,

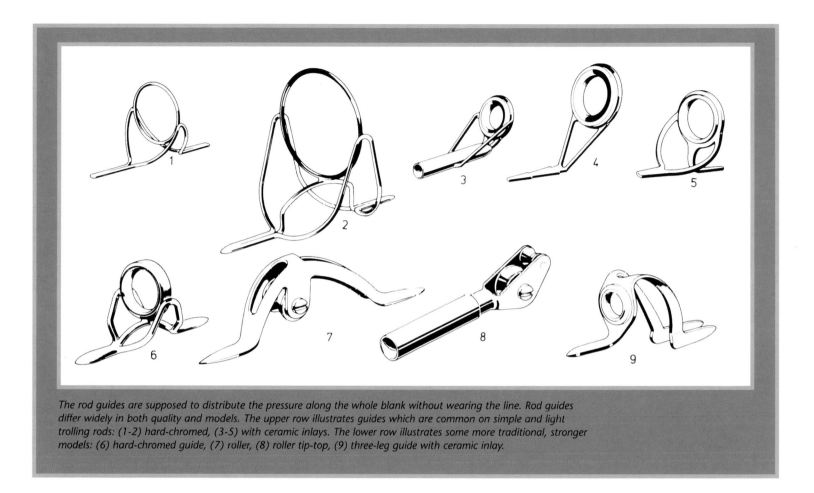

The rod guides are supposed to distribute the pressure along the whole blank without wearing the line. Rod guides differ widely in both quality and models. The upper row illustrates guides which are common on simple and light trolling rods: (1-2) hard-chromed, (3-5) with ceramic inlays. The lower row illustrates some more traditional, stronger models: (6) hard-chromed guide, (7) roller, (8) roller tip-top, (9) three-leg guide with ceramic inlay.

or in a gimbal cup on a fighting chair. The butt should also be made of extra-durable material – metal or graphite – since it is constantly subjected to wear and impact. When a rod is used without a rod belt, the butt should be covered with a rubber cap, to protect both your clothes and your body.

Rod guides

For many sportfishermen, the guides are a rod's hallmark of nobility. It is good advice, then, not to compromise when choosing them.

The task of the rod guides is to hold the line away from the blank, and to distribute the pressure over the whole rod without putting wear on the line. The friction between the line and a guide generates heat, so it is best for big-game fishing to use rollers that rotate as the line runs over them. This, of course, requires them to be kept free from salt deposits and other obstacles, so that they really spin well. On most trolling rods, a tip guide with a roller is a definite advantage.

Roller guides are not preferable, though, when the temperature falls below freezing, since they get plugged up with ice and become more troublesome than useful. Knots can also jam a roller. So always check that sizeable knots, such as a Bimini twist, can pass through the rod's roller and ring guides.

Other high-quality guides to choose among are made of silicon carbide, hardloy and aluminum oxide. Stainless-steel guides are still common on some saltwater rods. As for chromed guides, a line will eventually eat into them because of the salt on it. Tungsten carbide guides, commonly called "Carboloy" guides, are the answer for those who use a wire line. These guides, however, can damage ordinary lines, so a wire-line rod should be used with discretion. As a wire line is not elastic, the rod should be of the slow-action type.

Occasions arise when the trolling fisherman wants to have a rod of 10-15 feet (3-4.5 m) in the boat, for example when fishing with very light lines. A so-called "noodle rod", with rotatable guides, will dampen and compensate for the line's thickness, as well as the fish's leaps and rushes. Similarly, when harling is done from a small boat in a river, it may be desirable to reach out far with the gear – although not, in this case, with extremely light lines or light rods.

Reels

The basic points when selecting a reel for trolling are to be sure that it has enough line capacity for the intended fishing, and that it has a smooth drag which can take the heat of letting out line fast. It must also be able to tolerate a salty environment if used there. Another advantage, which I rank high, is a counter that shows how many yards or meters of line are out. This makes it easier, for instance, to place lures in a relative pattern.

The spinning reel

Trolling for pike, walleye and perch is the main use of a spinning (fixed-spool) reel. The equipment on board then tends to be sparse, as well as easier to supervise and to get at, than when trolling with a downrigger.

Among spinning reels, the Baitrunner or Live liner models are by far the best for trolling. When letting the line out and down, for example, the spool can be disengaged while the slip-drag is still working. In addition, one need not drop the bail in order to feed out the line. The drag is easy to set in advance and to adjust during the fight.

The revolving spool reel

Nine times out of ten, a revolving spool reel is perfect for trolling. A large bait-casting reel serves often as a good trolling reel. The pure trolling reels vary in size, shape and structure according to their purposes. In general, they are strongly built and saltwater resistant, with an ample drag system and a satisfying line capacity. Harness lugs, and an extra safety lock in the form of a clamp around the rod seat, are frequently standard. Reel sizes are numbered from 1/0 to 16/0, or marked with IGFA classes from 12 to 130.

The letter W after a rod's class means that it has an unusually wide spool for its size, and thus holds more line than a normal spool does. Two reels with the same apparent size may also have spools with different geometry and, therefore, line capacity.

You should always check that the spool tolerates the type of line to be put on it, since a tightly wound monoline, for example, may burst the spool gables when it tries to regain its normal length. A good rule is to have a layer of cotton line nearest to the spool axle, and then fill up with the actual line. Spools cast in one piece are strongest. Anodized aluminum and stainless steel are well-tried spool materials, but caution is needed with artificial fibers – even if these make the reel lighter. There should not be any free room between the spool and the reel gable, into which the line can risk sliding.

Line capacity

Inability to exploit all of the reel's line capacity is like going into a fight with a handicap. When the fish strikes, you already have some slack line out, and perhaps a lot if you are trolling with a downrigger. With little line left on your reel, the pressure on the line increases and the fish becomes harder to take home.

Reels have an enormous range of line capacities. And now, with thin, strong superlines, there is room on medium-class reels for a line capacity that a few decades ago was conceivable only on a big-game reel in the heavyweight class. For instance, a 50-class reel can hold about 750 yards of 50-lb monoline, but the same reel can take about 3000 yards of superline in the 50-lb class

Bait-casting reels, and the occasional small trolling reel, have line-spreaders. But no better and more durable level-wind than your own thumb has yet been designed for the heavier reels. Distributing the line with your thumb soon becomes a habit. The handle on a trolling reel should be large and provide a good grip even under very wet conditions. Its shape, though, is mostly a matter of personal taste and opinion.

The reel's gear ratio – how many times the spool rotates for every full turn of the reel handle – is another crucial detail. How much line is laid on the spool with each winding depends on the combination of gear ratio and spool diameter. The more line you have on the spool, the quicker you can take home line. An increasing number of trolling reels are two-speed reels. They come with two gears, mostly shifted with a button. The low gear winds in more powerfully, but it lays up less line on the spool for each turn than does the high gear.

Automatic gearing, which changes from fast to slow winding as the load varies, is used on some trolling reels in the light line classes.

Clicking and braking

A reel with little or no click (line-out alarm) is not a complete trolling reel. This sound is like an alarm clock to tell you that the moment has come at last – something is

Trolling reels vary in size, appearance and construction, depending mainly on the fighting characteristics of the expected prey, and on the conditions at the actual fishing place. The reel shown here is made for big-game fishing. Among other things, it has a lever drag, which is both easier and safer to handle than a star drag.

pulling line off the reel. So the clicking should be clear enough to be heard over the waves' slap and the motor's hum, when the rod is not in your hands. It will also enable you to prevent the spool from backlashing, and thus the line from over-winding if it is being let out when you disengage the spool.

The reel should be easy to take apart and put together – even on board, since you may have to change the spool or give it some other kind of service, possibly on a rolling boat deck. Regular maintenance by disassembling the reel, washing it clean, replacing worn parts and so on, is important in the world of big-game fishing. This is, of course, done most effectively and safely on land or in harbor. Always remember, after fishing, to reduce the drag, regardless of whether it is controlled with a lever or a star wheel. Otherwise, substances like salt may eventually destroy the drag discs, resulting in a jerky and unreliable drag.

Drags regulated by a star wheel have been responsible for catching thousands of world-record fish in all line classes. Nonetheless, they have been increasingly eclipsed by the lever-drag reels. These are easier to handle, brake better and last longer. On them, the spool and drag are coupled in by an arm which, on most reels, sits upon the winder gable.

Setting the drag

Always set the reel's drag for your fishing as soon as the reel is mounted and the line is drawn through the rod guides. And do it on land, not in a bouncing boat. Keep in mind that a drag is better set too loose than too tight. It is also both easier and safer, while playing the fish, to add extra braking with your thumb than to readjust the drag. With a trolling reel, though, there are some golden rules: the drag should be set to 15% of the line's breaking strength in lighter line classes, and to about 25% in heavier classes.

Years of experience give many fishermen an almost intuitive feeling for drag settings. By pulling the line with one hand and thumb-braking the spool with the other, they usually get it right. However, even the most practiced sportfisherman will use a spring-scale to make a more correct adjustment. It is best to let someone else hold the scale, then to knot the line directly in the scale's suspension hook. Next, set the reel's drag lever in the striking position, and keep the rod tip pointing toward the scale. Reverse and adjust the drag setting until it begins to slip at the desired weight figure.

Specific advice for the " perfect" drag setting is difficult to give, as it depends on things like the lure's water resistance, the boat speed, the hook size and, of course, the fish's striking behavior.

Fishing lines

For decades, trolling fishermen have made their choice among monofilament, dacron and wire lines. Roughly speaking, a quarter-century ago the deep troller preferred wire lines, the big-game fisherman dacron lines, and the "everyday troller" monolines for rivers, lakes and skerries. But this division is no longer valid. Increasingly, modern superlines are being used. The downrigger has made it possible to troll with monolines and light equipment at depths which, in the past, could hardly be reached with wire lines. And out on the ocean, modern monolines are now more common than dacron lines, while thin, strong superlines are making rapid advances.

In Europe, lines are usually rated by their diameter (in mm) and strength in kilograms, while in the USA and several other countries it is the line strength in pounds that you buy. Keep in mind that the line absorbs water while fishing; this certainly makes it more flexible, but also reduces its strength by up to 20% after only a few hours of continuous fishing. What also reduces the line strength could be knots.

On the whole, trolling fishermen need thin but strong lines with low visibility, low memory, high abravision resistance and good sensitivity. A non-stretchy line hooks better than a more elastic one. It does not, however, take hard jerks – which are frequent in trolling – as well as a stretchy one does. The stifness and the line diameter may also impede the lure's movement, but can be compensated with a leader of limp line and a loop knot close to the lure.

The line's diameter has an influence on how fast it sinks, how heavy a sinker is needed to reach a certain trolling depth, how much line can be laid on the reel, how clearly the line can be seen, and how easy it is to knot. The line's breaking strength, too, determines what equipment – such as rods – is chosen, how much drag can be set, and how far you can push the equipment during the fight. A thinner line makes a lure go deeper than a thick line does, since it creates less water resistance. For example, a lure goes much deeper if you let out 250 ft (75 m) of line instead of 80 ft (25 m). But it is a lot harder to make a hookup with a long line, because of the line's elasticity.

Hi-Vis or fluorescent lines allow better control over the line spreading. In addition, this type of line is easier to see while playing the fish – an advantage when you are fishing in the dark or want to see quickly which way the fish is rushing. Such lines may, however, yield significantly fewer bites than less visible lines do. One way to avoid this drawback, while keeping the line control, is to taper the line with a neutrally colored leader – such as fluorocarbon, which is virtually invisible under the surface – closest to the lure.

Line twisting can occur when a lure is dragged in the propeller wash – or if you have a poorly rotating swivel, or none at all. The twisting may soon render the line unusable; but if it is discovered in time, a trolling fisherman has a relatively good chance of solving the problem fast. Just take off the lure, swivel and so forth, then feed out the line from the reel into the wake of the moving boat. The line will untwist and regain its original condition automatically.

Before fishing, always check the line's condition for some distance along the spool, not just the outermost turns. You should therefore change, turn or splice the line if you have the slightest doubt about its durability.

Monofilament lines

What we commonly call monofil lines are termed by their makers – according to the manufacturing process – homopolymers, copolymers, tripolymers and cofilament. These words use "homo" for one, "co" for two, "tri" for three, and "polymer" for nylon. Thus, homopolymer is a uniform type of nylon, copolymer is a combination of two types, and tripolymer combines three types. These mixtures were invented to give a line as many good qualities as possible. Copolymer is most popular in trolling circles. It comes in test strengths from 1 lb to 400 lbs, and in several colors.

Big-game fishing brings real excitement. Not only the fisherman but also his equipment must be in perfect trim. The gear has to be well-balanced, with the rod, reel and line adapted to each other. This has led the IGFA to develop an internationally accepted line-class system, which makes it much easier to match the items of equipment. These classes are 2, 4, 8, 12, 16, 20, 30, 50, 80 and 130 lbs (1, 2, 4, 6, 8, 10, 15, 24, 37 and 60 kg). If you buy a trolling rod of IGFA class 10 kg (20 lbs), you should normally match it with a line and reel of the same class. A well-tended and balanced set-up will give the most fishing time and the fewest problems.

Fluorocarbon lines

In appearance, fluorocarbon lines are reminiscent of monoline. They are manufactured not from nylon, however, but from polyvinylidene fluoride, a material that is denser, has a harder surface and does not absorb water in the same way as a monoline. The major advantage with this line is its invisibility under water, a great advantage for trolling in clear water. With less stretch and diameter compared with a monoline in a corresponding class, come the added factors of high sensitivity to bites and hooking ability. Another plus is its durability and good tolerance for ultraviolet light. Such negative factors as stiffness and line memory – which have meant that up to now fluorocarbon lines were used primarily in lighter-weight classes of line and leaders – appear to have been eliminated with the new generation of fluorocarbon lines. There are even hybrid lines on the market, manufactured from nylon and fluorocarbon, in which the advantages of both have been successfully combined.

Dacron lines

A dacron line is spun from dacron fibers. It is hollow, which makes it suitable for splicing. This in turn can mean strong, smooth splices, which easily run over roller guides and through ring guides on a rod. One can also, of course, join dacron lines with knots. In general, the result is less durable than monofilament, and therefore only a few kinds of knots are considered to be reliable, but these provide almost 100% joining strength. However, dacron line is significantly more vulnerable to damage than monoline.

Superlines

Superlines are manufactured from a polyuthlene material that may be either braided or fused. Power Pro is an instance of the former variety, Fireline of the latter. Compared with a monoline, a superline has enormous strength in relation to its diameter, with the glued variant being somewhat thicker than the braided line for the same breaking strength. The fine diameter of the superlines means that they cut through the water with minimal resistance and also give the lure a lively gait. Further, the line's minimal stretch means that a bite is easily registered and the hooking can take place well. For someone unfamiliar with these lines, the minimal elasticity may result initially in a snapped line or the hook's being torn out of the fish's mouth. A monoline or fluorcarbon shocktip leader and a drag set lighter than usual can solve the problem.

Always bed the spool with monoline and then fill it with the desired length of superline, using the UNI knot to join super- and monolines. This and the Palomar Knot are good for connections to swivels, hooks and lures. The Bimini Twist is very useful for doubling the line. The new generation of superlines are streamlined and do not generate the same friction against the guides as older types of lines did.

Metal lines

Lead-core and solid steel lines, thanks to their high specific weight, can sink down to great depths even with very light lures. So they are a good alternative for fishermen who do not use either a downrigger, a diving planer, heavy sinkers, or long-lipped and deep-diving plugs.

Metal lines are stiff and therefore hook well, but they are also much harder to handle than other types of line. Remember that a metal line which has got caught in something, and been stretched, has been weakened as a result. But light rods with slow action, and shock leaders made of monofilament, make it easier to fish with metal lines.

Do not fill the spool with metal line alone; bed it near its axle with a layer of dacron line. Avoid using spools made of plastic – as well as aluminum spools, since in combination with metal lines they corrode very easily in salt water. The metal line that tolerates salt water best is Monel.

Lead-core line is the easiest to handle of all metal lines. However, it rusts in salt water and thus requires special care. As its own name indicates, it has a core of lead wire, around which dacron or nylon is spun. This casing gives it protection and strength, while the core makes it sink fast. Consequently, what increases in the heavier line classes is the size of the casing, not of the core. A heavier lead-core line actually sinks a little slower than a thin one, due to the water resistance. Most lead-core lines change in color every 3 ft (90 cm) or every ninth yard (meter), helping you to see how much line is let out.

Knots and joints

Not even an expensive and excellent line is worth putting between yourself and the fish unless your knots and joints are made with the greatest possible care and thought. Most significant for a trolling fisherman is the ability to join thin lines with thick ones, and to join lines that consist of different materials.

It is also important to be able to double a line in the right way, and then to knot it properly to a swivel. Equally essential is the knack of putting a leader on a hook and fashioning different variants of knots that suit the trolling fisherman's lures. He or she must, in addition, master the craft of the sleeve – both for monofilament and for wire lines – and of joining wire lines by hand, as well as coupling them to the hook and lure.

Some knots should become a part of you. These you must be able to tie with frozen fingers, in the dark, or on a rolling boat deck. It is therefore always best to tackle the equipment on solid land, before the boat leaves the harbor. Practice knots at home, tying them slowly and studying them in detail. Tighten a knot gradually and evenly, never with a jerk.

On most monofilament lines – except those with a very smooth surface finish – the knots become more durable if they are wet before being tightened. A good monoline knot should not slip. Dacron lines, on the other hand, are best joined by splicing or with a few special knots, as mentioned above.

A knot's reliability often depends on how many turns of line are wound into it. Be particularly careful to make the right number of turns, and check that they lie right and tight, so that the knot isn't weakened. A few knots can reach the same strength as an unknotted line and these should naturally be used if the situation permits.

The knots and leader models presented here are old and time-honored. They have been tested under varying conditions on different fish species all over the world, and – when tied right – they are 90% to 100% reliable. My advice is to learn all about the possibilities of the universal knot, which has proved its usefulness particularly in big-game fishing.

It is during the final stage of the fight that your equipment is really put to the test. Line, knots and joints should be among the least likely to break, if the fish is to be safely bagged as shown here.

The UNI knot system

This system has the advantage that, starting from one basic knot, you can vary it so much that the majority of knot problems faced by a trolling fisherman are readily solved. The fundamental UNI knot is one that has long existed in many countries. A corresponding number of names are given to it, but the usual one is its English name – the Grinner knot.

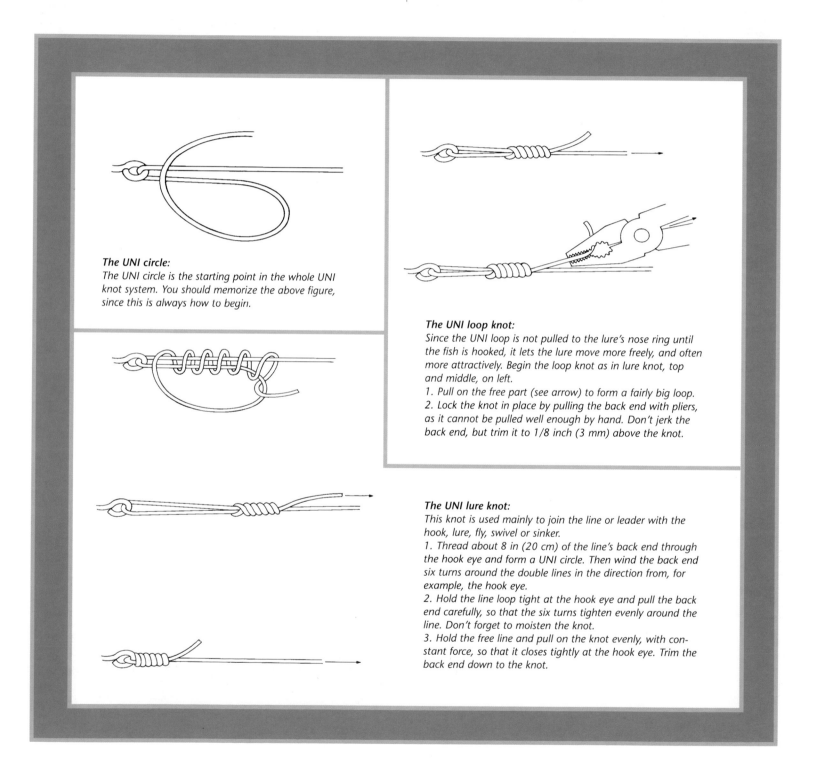

The UNI circle:
The UNI circle is the starting point in the whole UNI knot system. You should memorize the above figure, since this is always how to begin.

The UNI loop knot:
Since the UNI loop is not pulled to the lure's nose ring until the fish is hooked, it lets the lure move more freely, and often more attractively. Begin the loop knot as in lure knot, top and middle, on left.
1. Pull on the free part (see arrow) to form a fairly big loop.
2. Lock the knot in place by pulling the back end with pliers, as it cannot be pulled well enough by hand. Don't jerk the back end, but trim it to 1/8 inch (3 mm) above the knot.

The UNI lure knot:
This knot is used mainly to join the line or leader with the hook, lure, fly, swivel or sinker.
1. Thread about 8 in (20 cm) of the line's back end through the hook eye and form a UNI circle. Then wind the back end six turns around the double lines in the direction from, for example, the hook eye.
2. Hold the line loop tight at the hook eye and pull the back end carefully, so that the six turns tighten evenly around the line. Don't forget to moisten the knot.
3. Hold the free line and pull on the knot evenly, with constant force, so that it closes tightly at the hook eye. Trim the back end down to the knot.

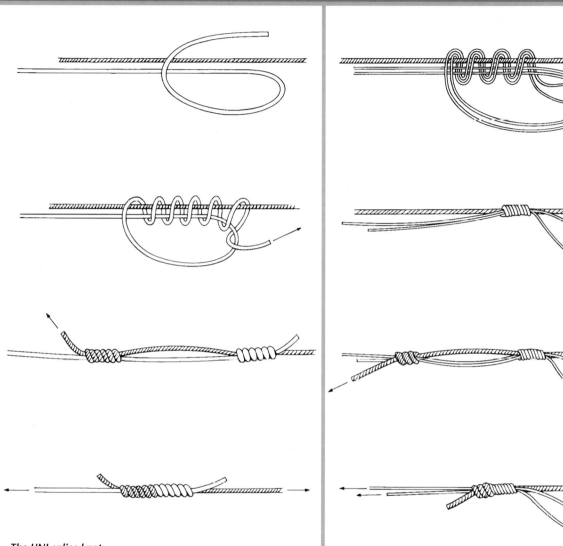

The UNI splice knot:
This knot is used to join two lines of about the same diameter. It is strongest if both line ends are doubled before tying the knot. For clarity, it is drawn here with single line ends.
1. Lay 8-10 in (20-25 cm) of the two lines' back ends parallel to each other. About midway along them, form one end into a UNI circle.
2. Wind the end six turns, as shown. Pull carefully until the turns tighten.
3. Do the same as in 1 and 2 with the other end. Now the knot should look as in drawing. Don't forget to moisten the knot.
4. Pull on both lines' free ends, so that they slide together and lock each other. Pull hard and evenly, then trim the back ends to about 1 mm above the knots.

The UNI leader knot:
This knot joins lines of different diameters, though their ratio should be at most 1 to 4. So if you fish with 0.30-mm line (breaking strength about 10 lbs or 4.5 kg), it should not be joined to a line thicker than 0.65 mm (about 40 lbs or 18 kg).
1. Double 10 in (25 cm) of line (not leader) and make a UNI knot as shown, 6 in (15 cm) from the leader, with four turns.
2. Close the turn by pulling on the double line's loop.
3. Form a UNI circle on the leader and make a 3-turn UNI knot around the leader and main line. Close the turn by pulling the leader's back end.
4. Moisten the lines and pull their back ends hard, so that the two knots slide together. Trim the ends down to the knots.

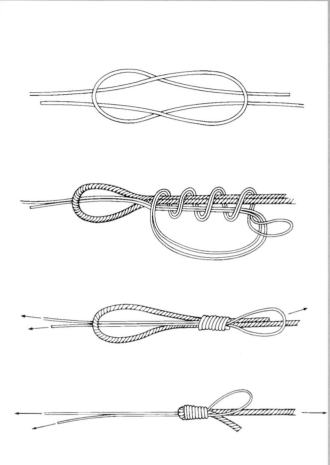

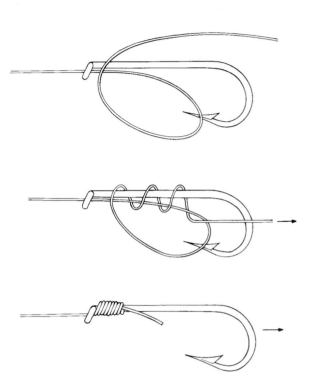

The UNI hook leader knot:

This knot is used to fasten the hook on the leader or main line.
1. Stick the line 8 in (20 cm) through a downturned hook eye. Hold the line against the hook shaft and form a UNI circle.
2. Tie a UNI knot around the hook shaft. Lay at least three turns and close them by pulling the back end.
3. Tighten the knot by pulling the main line and hook bend in different directions. Trim.

The UNI shock leader knot:

This knot is used when you need to join an extra thick and strong leader with the main line.
1. Double both line ends 10-12 in (20-25 cm). Stick the doubled main line's loop through the leader's loop, far enough to tie a UNI knot.
2. Form the UNI circle and wind the double main line four turns, as shown.
3. Close the turn by pulling on the main line's two ends with one hand, and on the loop with a forefinger.
4. Tighten the knot by pulling on the leader end with one hand, and on the main line's ends with the other hand. Pull slowly and evenly, not jerking. When the knot stops sliding, and the line turns are gripping properly around the leader at the loop, finish the knot by pulling both back ends. Trim well.

The UNI spool axle knot:

This knot is used to attach the line on the reel spool. On fly and spinning reels, the back end is laid around the spool before tying the knot. On fixed-spool reels, make a UNI loop and then tighten it around the spool axle.

The equipment and techniques of modern trolling have enabled ever more fishermen to be in the right place, at the right time, with the right method for hooking whatever they want.

Other types of knots

My complementary knots include the Bimini Twist, Spider Hitch, Albright Knot, Palomar Knot, Bristol Knot, Surgeon Knot and a swivel knot for double lines. You should also be familiar with splicing of different lines, with steel-line and wire sleeves, and with coupling of wires and monolines.

The Bimini Twist

This is a very handy and strong knot with up to 100% reliability. It is used chiefly to join leaders, and when doubling the main line above a terminal tackle. It is fairly easy to tie by yourself if the double line is not longer than 60 in (150 cm), but otherwise two people make the job both easier and safer.

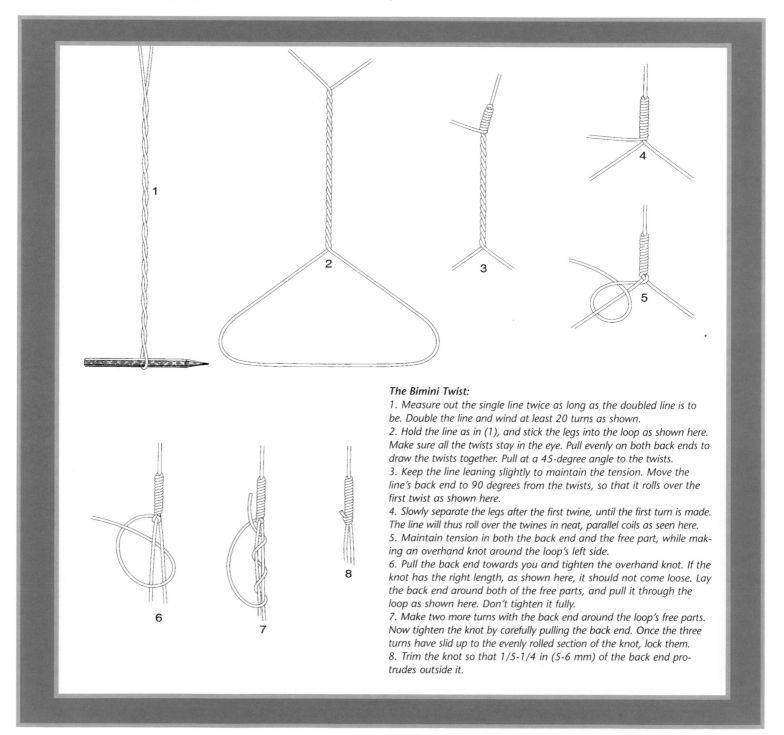

The Bimini Twist:
1. Measure out the single line twice as long as the doubled line is to be. Double the line and wind at least 20 turns as shown.
2. Hold the line as in (1), and stick the legs into the loop as shown here. Make sure all the twists stay in the eye. Pull evenly on both back ends to draw the twists together. Pull at a 45-degree angle to the twists.
3. Keep the line leaning slightly to maintain the tension. Move the line's back end to 90 degrees from the twists, so that it rolls over the first twist as shown here.
4. Slowly separate the legs after the first twine, until the first turn is made. The line will thus roll over the twines in neat, parallel coils as seen here.
5. Maintain tension in both the back end and the free part, while making an overhand knot around the loop's left side.
6. Pull the back end towards you and tighten the overhand knot. If the knot has the right length, as shown here, it should not come loose. Lay the back end around both of the free parts, and pull it through the loop as shown here. Don't tighten it fully.
7. Make two more turns with the back end around the loop's free parts. Now tighten the knot by carefully pulling the back end. Once the three turns have slid up to the evenly rolled section of the knot, lock them.
8. Trim the knot so that 1/5-1/4 in (5-6 mm) of the back end protrudes outside it.

The Spider Hitch

This knot can be tied fast, has high breaking strength, and can often replace the Bimini Twist in light line classes.

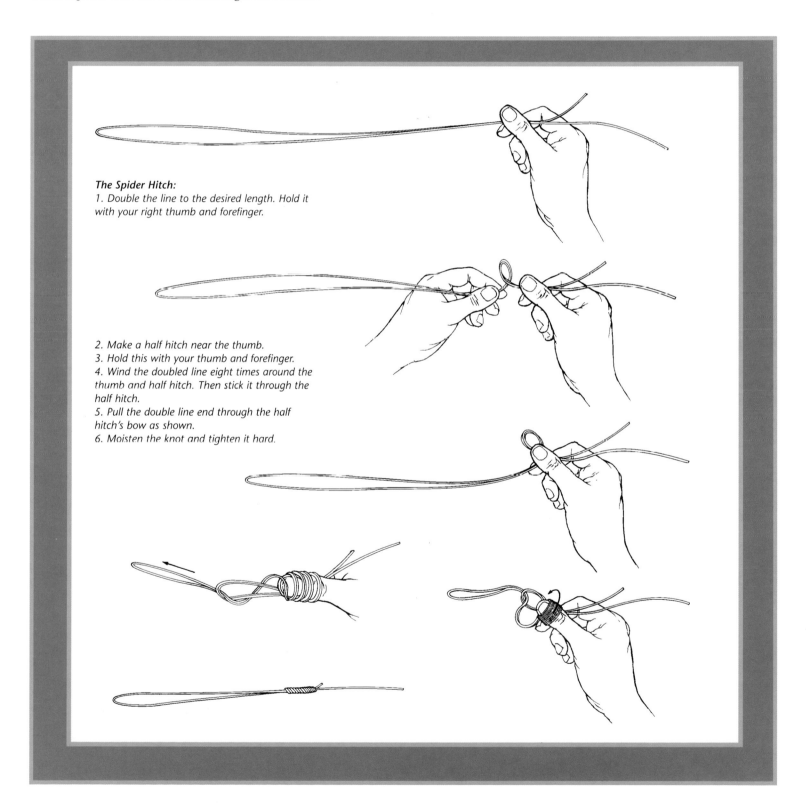

The Spider Hitch:
1. Double the line to the desired length. Hold it with your right thumb and forefinger.

2. Make a half hitch near the thumb.
3. Hold this with your thumb and forefinger.
4. Wind the doubled line eight times around the thumb and half hitch. Then stick it through the half hitch.
5. Pull the double line end through the half hitch's bow as shown.
6. Moisten the knot and tighten it hard.

The Albright Knot

This knot is used to join wire or thick monoline with, for example, thinner monofilament lines. When monolines are joined to solid wire, begin by making a "haywire twist" knot on the wire. Another use is when fishing without a swivel between the line and leader.

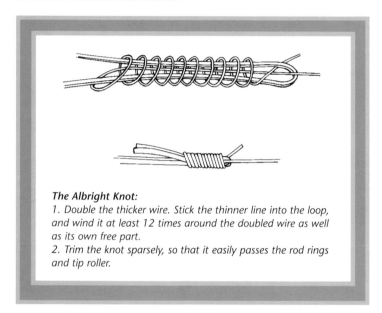

The Albright Knot:
1. Double the thicker wire. Stick the thinner line into the loop, and wind it at least 12 times around the doubled wire as well as its own free part.
2. Trim the knot sparsely, so that it easily passes the rod rings and tip roller.

The Surgeon Knot

This strong knot, easy and quick to tie, is used to unite two lines of the same or different dimensions. It is especially common for putting a leader on the line.

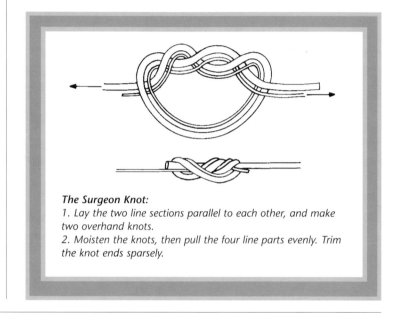

The Surgeon Knot:
1. Lay the two line sections parallel to each other, and make two overhand knots.
2. Moisten the knots, then pull the four line parts evenly. Trim the knot ends sparsely.

The Palomar Knot

A good knot to use with superlines.

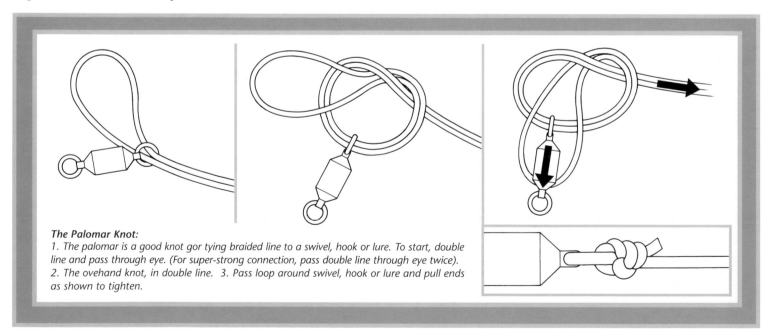

The Palomar Knot:
1. The palomar is a good knot gor tying braided line to a swivel, hook or lure. To start, double line and pass through eye. (For super-strong connection, pass double line through eye twice).
2. The ovehand knot, in double line.   3. Pass loop around swivel, hook or lure and pull ends as shown to tighten.

The Bristol Knot

A supple, strong, net knot for joins between double and single lines.

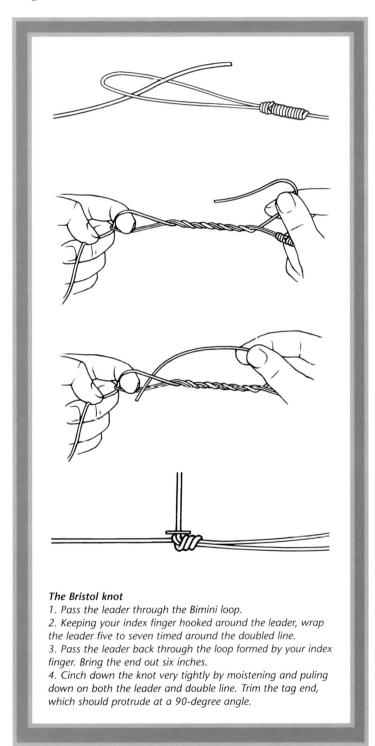

The Bristol knot
1. Pass the leader through the Bimini loop.
2. Keeping your index finger hooked around the leader, wrap the leader five to seven timed around the doubled line.
3. Pass the leader back through the loop formed by your index finger. Bring the end out six inches.
4. Cinch down the knot very tightly by moistening and puling down on both the leader and double line. Trim the tag end, which should protrude at a 90-degree angle.

The Swivel Knot

This knot is used to connect a doubled main line with the swivel.

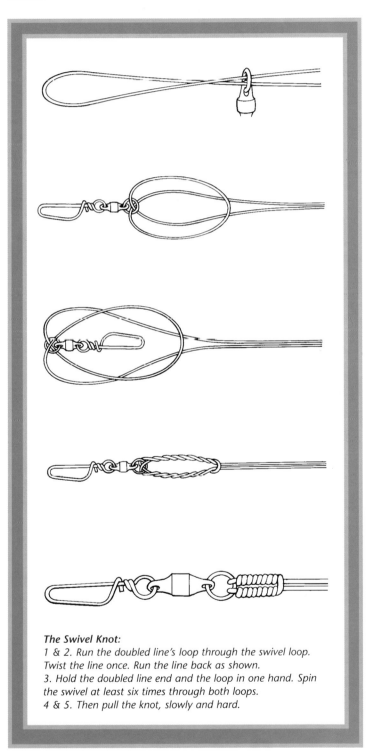

The Swivel Knot:
1 & 2. Run the doubled line's loop through the swivel loop. Twist the line once. Run the line back as shown.
3. Hold the doubled line end and the loop in one hand. Spin the swivel at least six times through both loops.
4 & 5. Then pull the knot, slowly and hard.

The Haywire Twist

This is the internationally name of the standard coupling between a solid wire and a hook, lure or swivel. It is also used when only a loop is made on a single-stranded wire.

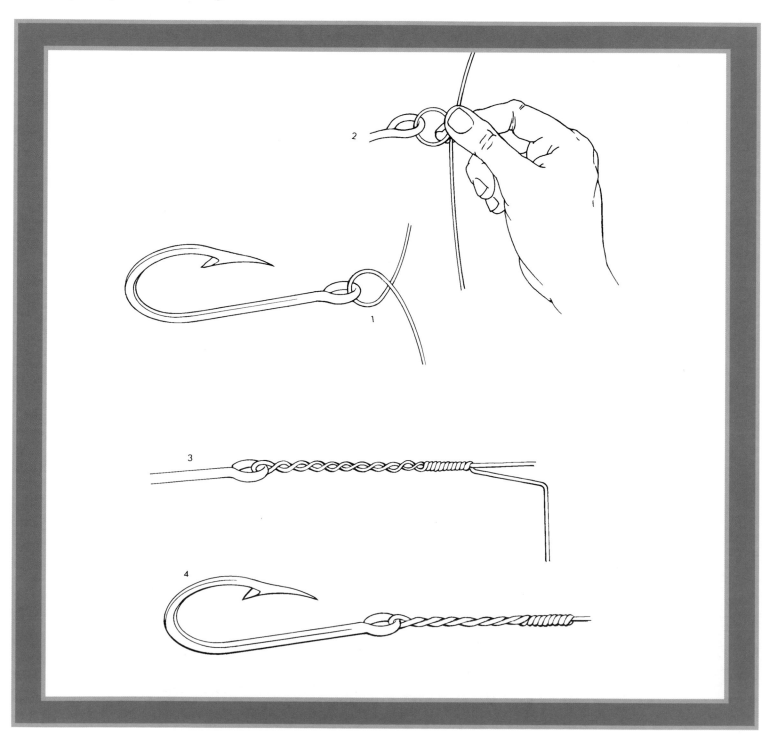

Sleeves

The commonest and easiest way to couple a multistrand wire line or heavy monoline to a hook, lure or swivel is to crimp one or more sleeves over the wire strands or line ends, using a crimping tool.

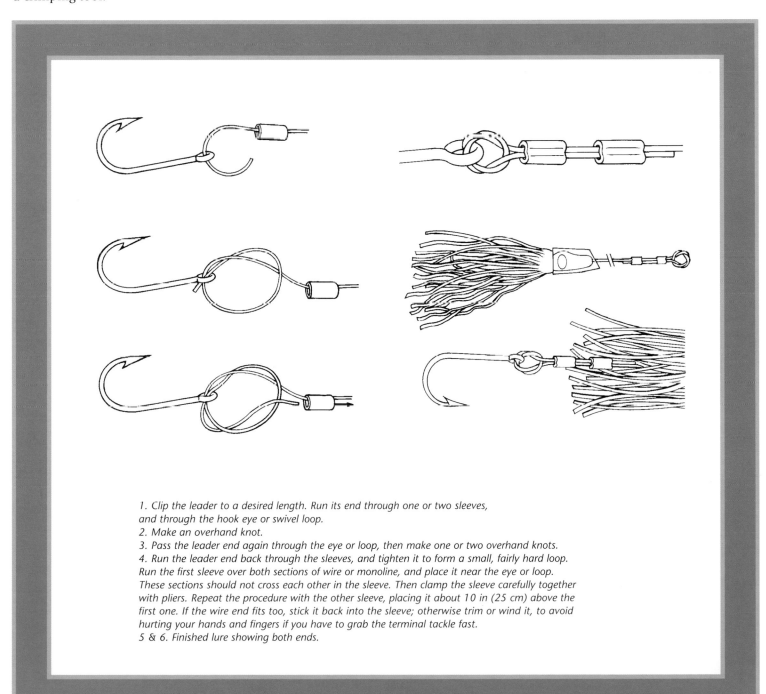

1. Clip the leader to a desired length. Run its end through one or two sleeves, and through the hook eye or swivel loop.
2. Make an overhand knot.
3. Pass the leader end again through the eye or loop, then make one or two overhand knots.
4. Run the leader end back through the sleeves, and tighten it to form a small, fairly hard loop. Run the first sleeve over both sections of wire or monoline, and place it near the eye or loop. These sections should not cross each other in the sleeve. Then clamp the sleeve carefully together with pliers. Repeat the procedure with the other sleeve, placing it about 10 in (25 cm) above the first one. If the wire end fits too, stick it back into the sleeve; otherwise trim or wind it, to avoid hurting your hands and fingers if you have to grab the terminal tackle fast.
5 & 6. Finished lure showing both ends.

Splicing

Dacron can be spliced to either monofilament line or dacron. A spliced line is usually weaker than an unspliced line, but the amount of weakening depends, for example, on how many dacron fibers have broken and how long the splice is. So the splice should be at least 4 in (10 cm) long, or 8-12 in (20-30 cm) for big-game fishing. Its advantage over a knot is that it is smoother and runs easier through loops, with less risk of getting caught at critical moments.

Monofilament to dacron

This simple splicing can make a long, smooth mono leader, which in the long run will tolerate friction and impact better than dacron line alone. Very different line diameters can be spliced.

1. Bend a piece of No. 2-4 fine steel wire, 2 yards (or meters long), into a sharp V-angle. Let us call this handy tool a "splicing needle".
2. Stick the V-bend into the hollow dacron line, about 2 yds (m) from the back end. Pull the dacron over the steel wire until the splicing needle comes out, though not so far that it slips off.
3. Sharpen about 4 in (10 cm) of the monoline's end with a razor blade.
4. Stick the monoline into the splicing needle. Monoline with a breaking strength of 100 lbs (45 kg), or a diameter over 1 mm, will be hard to get double through the dacron line. If so, stick the sharpened monoline into the end of a separate, thinner 30-lb dacron line, and seal the joint with glue.
5. Pull the splicing needle and monoline (with a 30-lb dacron line if needed) through the thicker dacron (reel) line, until the monoline emerges at the starting hole. Then clip off the monoline's sharpened end. Roughen a short part of the new end with sandpaper, drop a little strong glue on the monoline, and stick it into the reel line. Rub the joint smooth.
6. Wrap the "in and out" holes of the monoline with dental floss, for example, and cover the wrappings with strong glue. Then they will run perfectly.

Dacron to dacron

An efficient way to unite lines is with loops. But it is important for the lines to be coupled so that they do not cut each other (see the drawing). So on dacron lines, the loops are usually spliced.

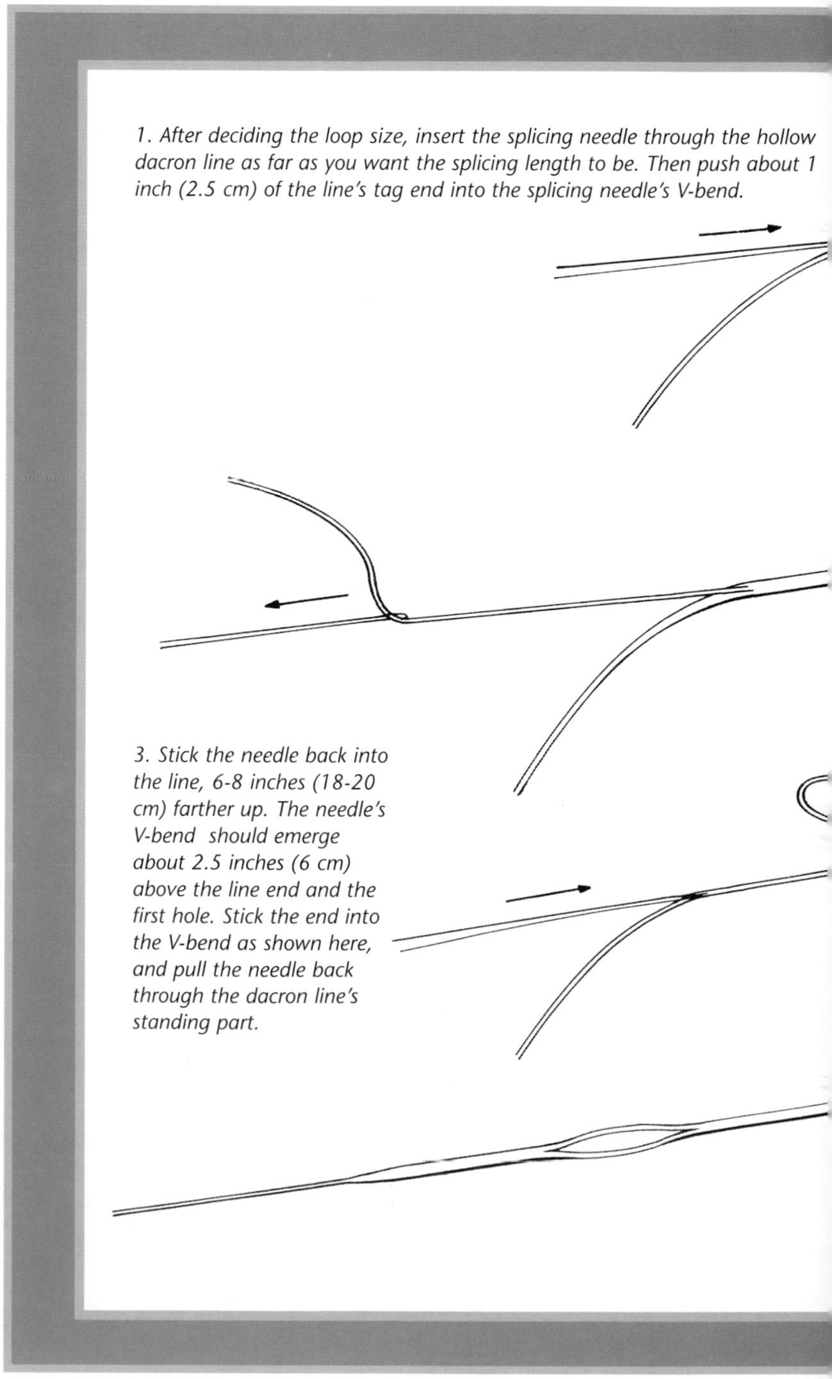

1. After deciding the loop size, insert the splicing needle through the hollow dacron line as far as you want the splicing length to be. Then push about 1 inch (2.5 cm) of the line's tag end into the splicing needle's V-bend.

3. Stick the needle back into the line, 6-8 inches (18-20 cm) farther up. The needle's V-bend should emerge about 2.5 inches (6 cm) above the line end and the first hole. Stick the end into the V-bend as shown here, and pull the needle back through the dacron line's standing part.

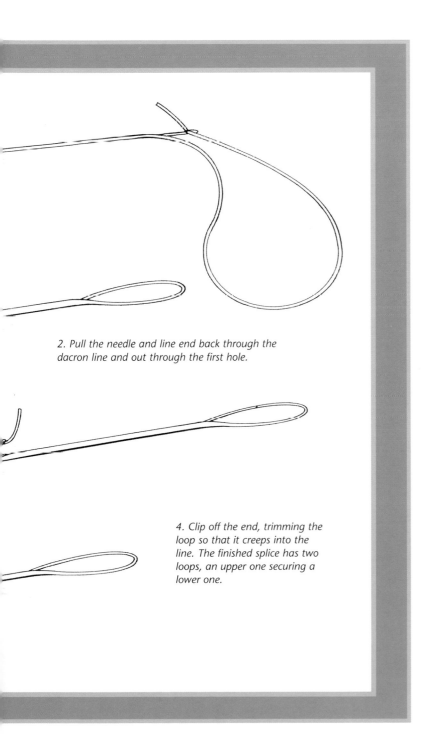

2. Pull the needle and line end back through the dacron line and out through the first hole.

4. Clip off the end, trimming the loop so that it creeps into the line. The finished splice has two loops, an upper one securing a lower one.

To a great extent, trolling involves teamwork. This is seen most clearly in big-game fishing, where the fisherman and crew have to work together in every respect if the catch is to be boarded.

Artificial lures

The trolling fisherman's jewelry casket is his tackle box, full of shiny shapes that seduce the fish and charm the sportsman himself. Some of these well-designed creations are not there to fish with, but simply because they were once effective and can be used to tell good tales about. Others may be so beautiful that one does not want to risk losing them by actually fishing with them.

A troller can normally use the same lures as a casting fisherman does. But he tends to choose specially designed lures, which are dominated less by weight than by their color and form. His starting point, however, is the same: they must be suited to the given equipment, fish species, and fishing environments. Thus he may open his box and pick out a plug, spoon, spinner, hair or plastic lure, a fly or squid imitation, or an offshore lure. Within each group, the lures vary according to shape, color, length, weight and movement.

The equipment on board should remain accessible but be protected and unobtrusive. Here the lures are hung up visibly in vinyl pockets, a tackle-keeper variant which is becoming increasingly popular among boat fishermen.

You shouldn't fall for a lure just because its color and shape please you. Check carefully that the surface finish, hooks, rings and swivels are of good quality, and that they can take the stress of the environment and fishing situations you may encounter. Always sharpen the hooks before these go overboard. Frequently even new lures – and especially big ones – have hooks that need filing or whetting. And don't exchange a single hook for a triple one, or a smaller for a larger one, without thinking: such measures can have a negative effect on the movement of the lure. An unsuitable swivel, or a stiff knot, may also ruin a lure's motion. It is often worth giving the lure room for play with a loop knot.

It is very important for a trolling fisherman to learn how different lures move at various speeds, so that he can match lures properly with each other. Running a high-speed lure alongside a normal, slowly wiggling spoon will mean, at best, that one of the lures is drawn forward at a good pace. Therefore, when letting out a lure, always check first from the boat's side that it has the expected movement in the water. Unequal line thicknesses and lengths can make two identical lures move differently.

The rod tip's rhythm frequently enables a seasoned fisherman to see whether the lure is running right. Some lures – such as stick plugs, jigs and flies – definitely run best if they are constantly influenced by rod movements with the hand. Keep in mind that certain lures are relatively insensitive to speed, and run attractively at both slow and fast speeds. Besides, what a marlin troller calls slow speed may be a maximum speed, or even more, for a salmon fisherman.

In addition, the light's angle and the water's depth have an influence on the visibility of colors underwater. How far down the light can penetrate depends on the season, time of day, and whether it is a sunny or cloudy day. Not for nothing do we speak of "sunshine plugs" and "gray-weather lures". The microorganisms around a lure may also reflect colors from it, making it more visible at times. Fluorescent colors are the most visible, especially fluo chartreuse.

Why a lure works one day and fails the next is an eternal, limitless question. But it can be partly answered if you keep a careful fishing journal. Record when, where, and how the fish strike; give meteorological and hydrological details about individual catches. Then your chances of being in the right place at the right time, with the right equipment, will be considerably enhanced.

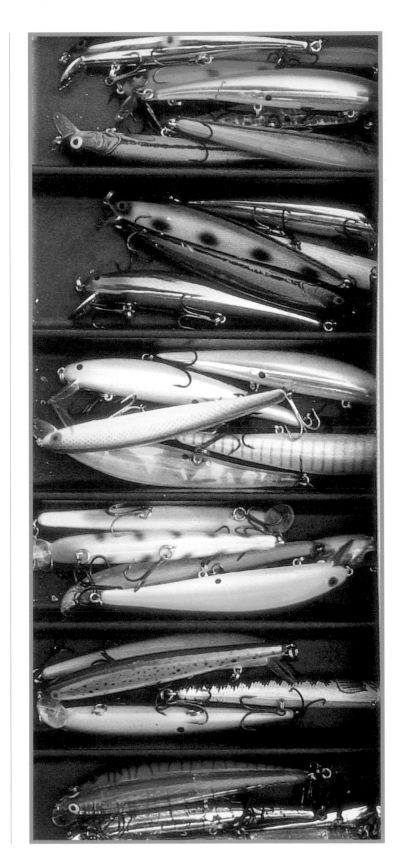

Plugs

A plug is usually designed to look like a bait fish, and classi-fied according to how deep it goes: there are surface, bottom, and deep types. As a rule, though, all of them occur in both floating and sinking versions.

Trolling plugs are comparatively light-weighted, in relation to their sizes of 0.8-14 in (2-35 cm). You can get a good idea of a plug's properties by inspecting the lip, the nose design and the body form. If the nose is angled downward, it tends to dive; if it is cut upward, it tends to rise. Cigar-like plugs do not arouse much attention with their run, but have to be set in motion with the rod tip, or by varying the boat speed. Among other tricks to stimulate the senses of fish are using plugs with two-part bodies, rattling beads in their bodies, or a small propeller at each end.

We generally speak of fast-beating and slow-wiggling plugs, referring to how they make their way through the water. The first type moves with short sidewise throbs that cause rapid vibrations. The second has a more sweeping gait, whose vibra-tions are also powerful but less busy in tempo.

The hook arrangement varies, of course, between different plugs. Depending on the size, it may be anything from a sin-gle hook to three treble hooks. Rapala's 10-in (26 cm) Magnum plug, for instance, has two very strong double hooks. Usually the hooks sit on rings in the body's fixed loops. But on some models, like the J-plug, the hook hangs free on a line that runs at an angle through the plug's body.

Spoons

The spoon is an age-old kind of lure. Tribes around the world have fashioned it from bone and shell for thousands of years. Modern spoons are usually made of metal, but plastic has gained ground even here.

A spoon's range of sizes is about 0.4-12 in (1-30 cm). The really big ones, have brought everything from monstrous Scandinavian pike to the billfish of southern latitudes along-side sportfishing boat sides.

The flashing reflectors of a big spoon can give predatory fish the impression of a fleeing school of prey. Most com-

Shape, color and weight are best varied when you select a set of lures. But don't keep too many lures in the same compartment. Otherwise they hook together and waste your time and temper when changing them on board. Besides, corrosion inside the tackle box may result.

Spoons are most popular among salmon-trolling fishermen. Some of the leading models are illustrated here.

monly, though, the wagging run of a spoon is supposed to imitate the movement of one baitfish. The surface of a spoon may be ball-hammered or bent in a special manner, to create strong reflections. A simple means of giving color to a gold, silver, or bronze-hued lure is to add multicolored stripes on it.

Some spoons are provided with one or more thin steel wires over the hook, which protect the hook from grass and other vegetation to minimize bottom-snagging.

Long thin spoons are more active in their movements than broad ones, which tend to swing wide when being trolled slowly. There are three general types of sheet-metal spoons: thick, medium and thin. A thick model is also commonly used to cast with. Many spoons of this type are excellent for surface trolling, as their own weight takes them down to the desired depth. But a large spoon has the disadvantage that the fish often manages to escape, because of the lure's weight and the abrupt break between the hook and spoon. A solution

here is to use a through-running tackle. The spoon slides up a little way along the line, giving a different load when the fish turns or leaps.

The medium type of spoon has a sheet-metal thickness of 0.02-0.035 in (0.5-0.9 mm). It seldom weighs more than 1/3 ounce (10 grams), so it usually needs help to get down to the chosen depth. This is done most simply by placing a sinker 1-2 yds (m) in front of the spoon.

The thin type, called a flutterspoon, of metal only 0.004-0.016 in (0.1-0.4 mm) thick, is incredibly light. It comes in short wide and long thin versions, according to the baitfish you want to imitate. A flutterspoon is easy to mangle so that, by varying the boat speed, you can make it resemble a wandering little fish that has been injured. Such a feather-light spoon should be fished on a short line of about 2 yds (m) from a diving planer or downrigger, to avoid losing its attractive fluttering movements.

A very important point, when using the lighter spoons, is not to overdimension the hook, swivels and snaps, rings, or the leaders line diameter. It can also be beneficial to exchange a triple hook for a single one.

A spoon is more sensitive to speed than some plugs are, and less tolerant of fast trolling boats. On the other hand, you can often troll slowly with a spoon. The right combination of spoon type and boat speed should be memorized thoroughly.

Spinners

The majority of trolling fishermen keep a set of spinners in their tackle box. Except for those seeking only bass, walleye, perch and char, the less commonly used of all lures are spinners.

This does not mean spinners are bad at catching fish; it shows, rather, that they are customarily thought difficult to troll with. In trolling circles, a spinner is seen as the worst line-twister in the lure box, and its reputation takes time to restore – even among the sportfishermen who, in other respects, are always considered eager to test both new and old techniques.

A spinner does not imitate prey fish, but attracts by virtue of its vibrations, reflections and colors. These are strengthened with hair, rubber, and plastic skirts – or, on some models, with plastic copies of worms and fish. Now and then, the hook is tipped with natural bait.

The blade on a spinner may be short and wide, or long and thin, with a choice of surface finishes. Mother-of-pearl blades are rated highly by many Scandinavian trollers for big char. Short, wide spinner blades can rotate most easily, whereas long thin ones require greater speed in order to spin and be heard.

So-called spinner lures look like a cross between a spinner and a jig. The blade or spoon sits on an arm made of steel wire, and wags forward over the jig head. Other models can carry natural bait such as small fish or worms on the single hook behind its leaden head and spinner blade..

Spin-N-Glo is another admired model, whose ample body with soft plastic wings can also rotate around a wire axle. Like other light spinners, it tends to be most assertive as the last outpost on a cowbell line.

Lures of hair and plastic

Hair lures are among the very oldest artificial lures known to man, while plastic lures are the latest to enter the field. This type of lure is mainly a visual attraction, due to its gait

or colors. Some fishermen also heighten the fish's interest by creating smells and sounds. There are lures which need to be continually worked so that their movements do not die out at times.

In fresh water, plastic lures are more popular for casting than for trolling. But in salt water, they are extremely popular with trollers. The largest ones of this kind, such as kona heads, will be discussed under offshore lures.

Hair and feather lures

Either traditional flies, or lures that imitate insects or bait fish, can be made of hair or feathers. So can Japanese feathered jigs. While the first kind need help to reach fishing depths, the last kind sink by their own weight.

The materials of modern hair and feather lures are partly natural and partly synthetic. They may be durable as well as delicate, and can be made either to pulsate heavily or just to glimmer.

In size, material, and other features, these flies and lures are adapted to the water and fish species. A harling fisherman (back troller) should thus have a wide range of them in order to match the shifting conditions, sometimes quite rapid, of river fishing. On the other hand, a marine fisherman's feather lures take more punishment and are chosen in terms of quality rather than quantity.

Plastic lures

The advent of soft plastic introduced " exact" copies of fish, crustaceans, reptiles, mollusks and invertebrates. Certainly the animals most often imitated in these groups are worms. This does not mean they are the commonest in trolling circles, where I would say that squids outnumber all others.

Trolling fishermen, though, have far more enthusiasm about plastic lures in fish form. The fast-vibrating tail of a fish body, on a single hook behind a small jig head, is attractive even to human eyes. Larger plagiarisms of mullet, flying fish and ballyhoo have often been profitable in big-game fishing, when they tempt the appetites of billfish.

Squid copies, as mentioned, are highly praised in all trolling environments. They rate strongly even in waters where the fish have never seen a squid. There are pure copies of octopi, squid and cuttlefish in natural colors – but also very simple, cowl-like models with huge luminous eyes in fantastic colors. Their length varies between 0.8 and 12 inches (2-30 cm).

Colorful, big-eyed plastic lures are conquering ever more expanses of trolling water. This is a diverse collection including, at lower right, some "birdies" - teasers that are dragged in the surface and arouse the curiosity of fish.

These imitations can be draped over natural bait as well as artificial lures, or the hook can be directly tipped with them. Normally, colorful beads or special lead sinkers are placed under the cowl.

Plastic lures are generally inexpensive and need not be used sparsely. They can save a lot of fishing days over difficult bottoms. Since some variants are not very durable, one should check that their dressings can stand being dragged and worn before one tosses them overboard.

Soft plastic can destroy a tackle box unless it is "wormproof", meaning that it tolerates the acid which some plastic lures give off.

Offshore lures

All lures used in the big-game arenas of the oceans can be called offshore lures. They might be Rapala's Magnum plug, Pelagic´s Modulure, ABU-Garcia's giant plastic eels, or big-eyed plastic-skirted lures with hard or soft plastic heads such as the Kona Head, Hooker Softhead and Calcutta.

In this multifaceted realm of constant innovations, the last type is most familiar. It is what we usually mean by offshore lures. Including bibless lures as Modulure and Marauders they also go by the name of high-speed lures, as some of them can take more than 20 knots. On average, they are used at 8-10 knots. But their size, weight and, in

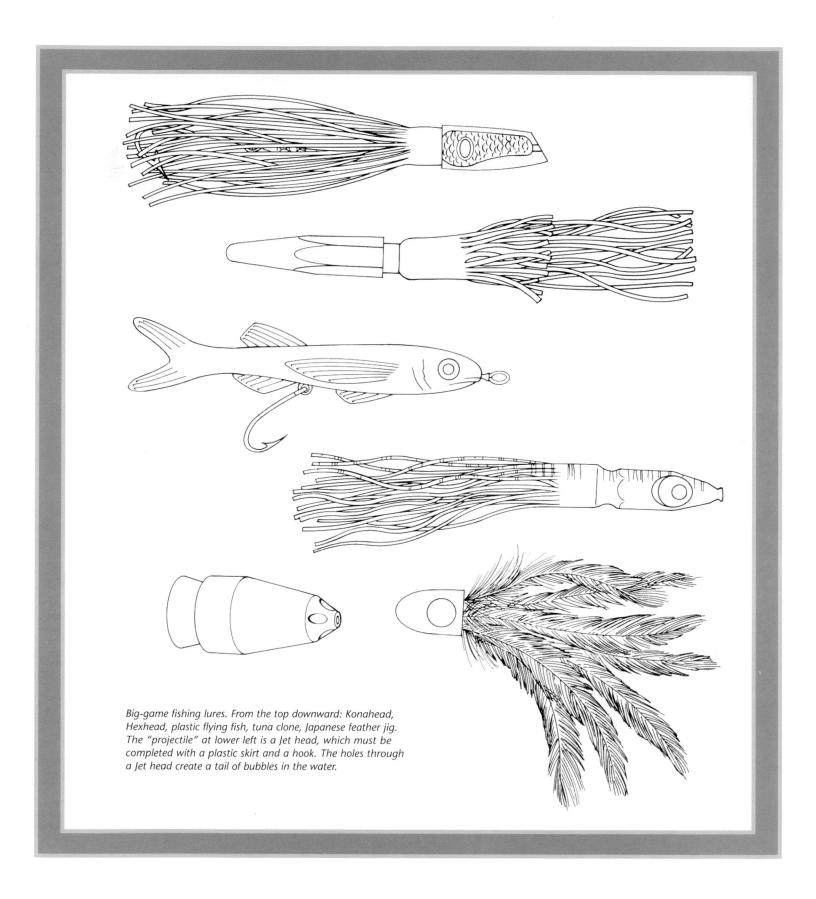

Big-game fishing lures. From the top downward: Konahead, Hexhead, plastic flying fish, tuna clone, Japanese feather jig. The "projectile" at lower left is a Jet head, which must be completed with a plastic skirt and a hook. The holes through a Jet head create a tail of bubbles in the water.

particular, head form are what determine how fast these lures can be trolled, as well as how they move through the water.

Many of them have to go just under the surface and leave a wake of bubbles, or "smoke", after them. They should not break the surface, though the bubble wake can very well raise spray behind them. It is also worth trying to keep the lure on the stern wave's front – the side turned towards the boat. Size, color and model are to be varied within the chosen trolling pattern.

Most fishermen prefer having the liveliest lures closest to the boat, and calm ones farther out. The latter are mainly supposed to attract billfish and tuna, whereas smaller models tend to draw the majority of pelagic sportfish – such as wahoo, yellow mackerel, albacore, bluefish, Pacific and Atlantic salmon.

Offshore lures come in sizes of 4-16 in (10-40 cm). They are sold in diverse colors, both tackled and untackled, with wire or thick monoline, and with single or tandem hook arrangements. The hook is hidden under a fringed plastic skirt, which may be partly made of mylar or pearl bands. The wire or monoline always runs through the head of an offshore lure. As a result, the hole's entrance puts extra wear on the line. With some variants – such as Kona Heads, which are relatively mobile – the wire or line should be checked frequently and carefully.

Normally, offshore lures are big-eyed; some have movable pupils and, in their heads, rattling beads. They are usually identifiable by their head form, classified as flat-faced or scoop-like or torpedo-shaped.

With the exceptionally resistant Modulure plug for sharp-toothed fish, it is possible to change pattern cards in its body, thereby easily testing the day's most marketable color and pattern.

Speed data

As we know already, trolling fishermen have vastly different ideas of what are slow, medium and fast speeds - depending as a rule on the fishing place and species. For instance, salmon trollers consider three knots to be fast, while a tuna troller regards it as slow. The following definitions are due to discussions with sportfishermen around the world:

Designation	Fresh water	Salt water
Slow speed	0-1.7 knots	0-4 knots
Medium speed	1.8-2.6 knots	4-8 knots
Fast speed	2.7-4.2 knots	8-12 knots
Ultrafast speed	4.3-5.2 knots	12-22 knots

Taking the fresh-water definitions as a basis, some of the most popular artificial lures fall into the groups given below. As can be seen, certain lures are both "strollers" and "sprinters", with a wider speed tolerance than others have. Your own trimming or loading of lures may also make them cross the lines between groups.

Slow speed

Spoons: Sutton, Miller's, Enforcer, Evil Eye, Toby, Utö, Siljan, Apex Hot Spot.
Wobblers: Bomber, Rebel, Rapala, Flatfish, Swim Whizz, Gladsax.
Flashing attractors: mini-cowbells with worms, dodgers with plastic lures and hair flies.
Spinners: Mörrum Spinner, Vättern Mother-of-Pearl, Vibrax Minnow, Mepps Giant Killer, Mepps Aglia, Wally Spin, Buzzer.

Medium speed

Spoons: Toby, Atom, Glimmy, Mörtblänk, Siljan, Professor, Lättke, Storauren, Möresilda, Landa Lukki, Crocodile, Rebel Arrowhead, Loco, Ingö, Apex Hot Spot, Evil Eye, Diamond King, Northern King, Northport Nailer, Southport Slammer, Flutter Chuck (Magnum, Big Ed), Piraten, Finn-Weaver.
Wobblers: ABU Hi-Lo, Cisco Kid, Killer, Rapala, Rebel, Bomber, Bagley Top Gun, Swim Whizz, Nils Master Invincible, J-plug, Jensen, Gladsax.
Flashing attractors: large dodgers, flashers with plastic lures and hair flies.

Fast speed

Spoons: Toby, Landa Lukki Turbo, Evil Eye Monarch, Piraten 66, Northern King (28, Magnum), Flutter Chuck Magnum, Rebel Arrowhead.
Wobblers: J-plug, Bomber Long A., Rebel Fastrac, Rapala (Original, Husky, Magnum, Shad Rap, Sliver), Nils Master Invincible, Cordell Ratt 1 Spot, Bagley Banger, Storm Thunderstick.
Plastic and feather lures: Hooker Softheads, Witch Doctor, Samurai feathers, Tube eels.

Natural baits

In fresh waters, the vast range of fish-like, convenient and effective artificial lures is seemingly gaining ever more ground over natural bait. This is an ominous trend, since natural baits – if used properly – are just as good as in the past. And they're definitely some of the most useful items a hook can be stuck in. Comparisons between salmon catches in the Great Lakes and on the west coast of North America are also clear evidence for the advantages of natural bait.

The salty environment, especially in big-game fishing, is indisputably ruled by natural baits in many places. Bait rigging is still regarded there as an art, and the people who master this work with knife, needle and thread enjoy high status among the world's fishing globetrotters and charter-boat skippers. They harbor no doubt that a well-sewn, well-balanced natural bait is unbeatable when it comes to attracting balky giants.

You can find natural baits in dried, frozen, fresh and living variants. The species are numerous, but a minority of them predominate in fresh, brackish and salt waters alike. Mackerel, ballyhoo, mullet, herring and squids are a strong quintet of baits in the sea. Nightcrawlers, smelt, vendace, and some of those mentioned above are the leaders in fresh and brackish waters.

These baits are not equally suitable for being served in the given form. But normally you obtain the bait stripped or slabbed, or else as a half or whole fish. One basic rule is that the bait should not be too big for the predator to swallow quickly. Another is that the hook(s) should always be as sharp as possible.

Even for a practiced bait-rigger, some time is needed to sew a trolling bait together. An alternative to sewing – as far as small whole fish or filets are concerned – can be to use a bait holder. The bait is usually clamped or pierced into the holder, which is shaped to protect the bait as well as giving it an attractive movement.

Baits are generally prepared before one leaves the harbor, and preserved in a way that keeps them fresh until they are used. A method of preserving fresh – or recently thawed – baits is to lay them in plastic bags, possibly with coarse salt, and then on ice. Avoid freezing a bait that has already been used or frozen.

Remember that live baits cannot be trolled as fast as dead ones. The maximum speed for a live trolling bait is around 4 knots, which saltwater fishermen define as slow. In big-game arenas, though, dead baits are trolled at up to 12 knots.

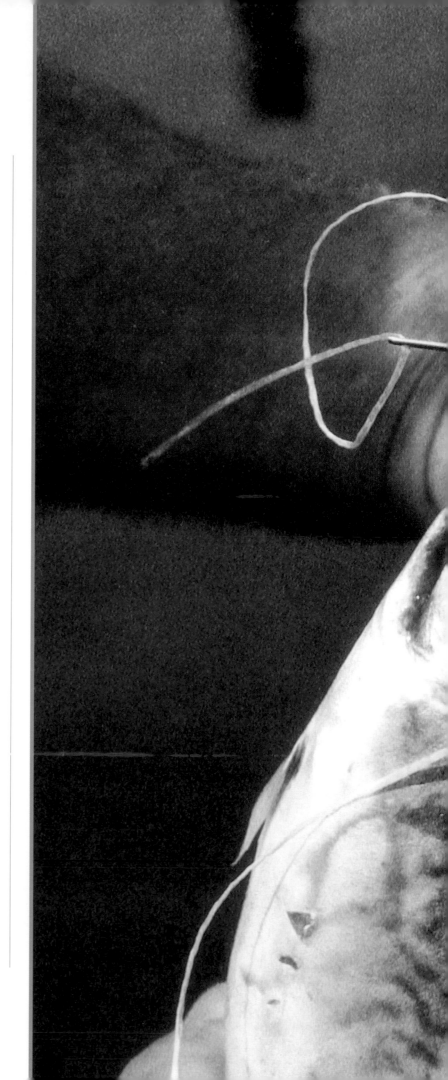

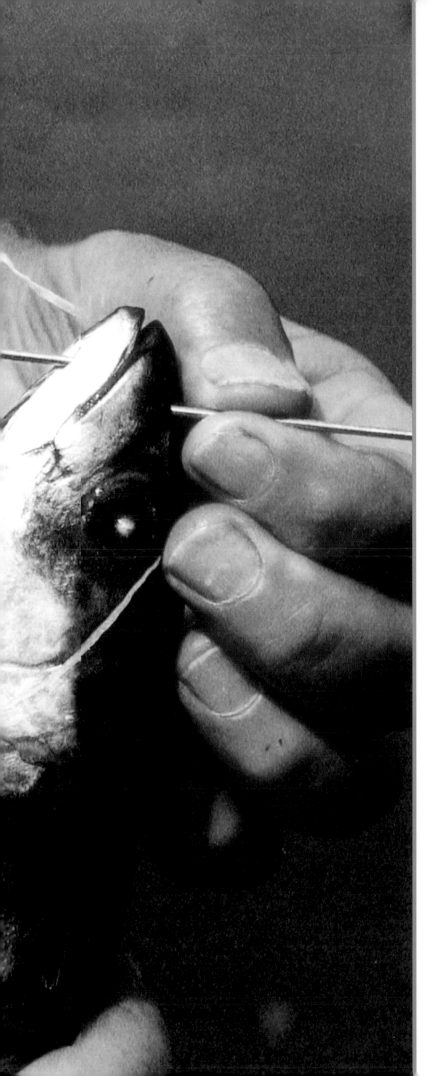

Stripping and slabbing.

A strip bait is undressed down to the bare skin. This is a very ancient kind of bait, easy to cut and preserve, as well as durable in use. It is effective in all trolling environments – whether on the edges of ocean canyons in strips 1 ft (30 cm) long, or on perch shallows in patches 1-2 in (3-5 cm) long. There is no trouble in coloring or dressing it by pulling a very short plastic skirt over it. An additional advantage is that it hooks well, mainly because it is soft and readily swallowed.

The best strip baits come from fish in the mackerel family, which have firm flesh and can be cut easily. Many other strip baits, such as a belly strip from a perch, can be amazingly effective – especially when fishing for their own family. With mackerel fish, too, it is from the belly or side that the 8-12 in (20-30 cm) long, tapering pieces are taken for big-game fishing.

A feather-like shape is best, so that the head end of the bait becomes wider than the tail part. The latter can also be slit. Cut away most of the flesh. Only after these cuts, and the insertion of a well-balanced Kirby hook, does the strip bait acquire its bold, attractive movement. If this does not look right, the reason may be that the hook and leader are not quite centered, or that the bait has slid down over the hook.

Slab baits, on the other hand, are usually wedge-like pieces that have been cut crosswise from a mackerel filet. The hook is pushed through the thick, fleshy part and out through the skin. This bait is fished slashing in the surface, normally without the aid of a sinker.

Left: Bait tackling is a difficult and enviable art to master. Many big-game fishermen and charter-boat captains say that the real difference between a successful fishing day, and a failed one, lies in the ability to handle bait with a knife, needle and thread. The baits are presented in many shapes and sizes. Unless alive, they are normally prepared in advance and kept on ice.

Below: Strip baits - cut from the belly, sides or back of small prey fish related to mackerel - are excellent both as attractors and as natural bait.

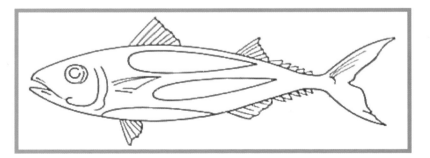

Whole fish

Offered either live or dead, whole fish vary in size according to the predator. In general, though, large trolling baits are more often live than dead. Mackerel, bonito, and bluefish are among the bigger and most popular variants. There are also many ways of rigging whole bait. Its size, firmness, condition and, to some extent, the water depth where it will be presented are the primary factors.

A live bait that is trolled slowly can stay alert for a very long time. The idea is that it should act as naturally as possible, but still send out signals which show that something is wrong. Surface-towed baits last longer than deep-running ones, and pollock tend to survive deep dives better than mackerel.

The rigging itself is important, too. Always use the smallest possible hook(s). The commonest method of rigging up small live baits is to place the hook in the mouth and up through its top jaw. Another is to run the hook through the nose-hole. On larger baits, a piece of dacron line is often threaded through the eye-hole and tied to the bend on a hook, which is secured around the fish's head. This is called a bridle rig and can be done quickly with a little training.

Big dead baits are ordinarily nose-rigged with a hook and dacron line. Herring and other small baits are frequently hooked through the body and given a double-hook arrangement.

Mullet

Gray mullet is a top-ranked bait. Variants in silver and black, as well as sizes of 2.5-25 oz (75-750 grams), are used in different circumstances. Mullet is called for when the sea is choppy, and silver mullet weighing 3-8 oz (100-250 grams) is especially popular in flatline fishing for the smaller billfish, such as sailfish.

By rigging the bait in diverse ways, you can also vary its behavior. Rigging it without a sinker will skip it on the surface. But to swim just under the surface, it should carry a sinker right below the jaw. A sinker over the nose produces a diving version. The spine is always removed, and this is best done with a deboner.

If the mullet starts to spin, it may be because the hook is sitting too tight or the sinker – if any – is not centered.

Ballyhoo

Many sought-after sportfish eat ballyhoo, which is therefore a much-appreciated bait. It swims in considerable schools near the surface, chiefly in tropical waters. Easily accessible and all-round in use, it is most popular in weights of 3-8 oz (100-250 grams). Ballyhoo serves as a skip bait, and can be frozen and thawed without trouble. A sign that it is fresh, and thus acceptable as bait, is that it still has its dark-blue to black color across the back.

Herring

Herring are pelagic fish and move in enormous schools through the Atlantic, Baltic and Pacific. The extent and spawning times of these stocks vary, as do their migration routes. Bait sizes are commonly 4-12 in (10-30 cm). This is an essential basic food for the mackerel, salmon and cod families. Fat and silvery, it should be as fresh as possible. Herring keeps for a fairly long time on ice, but it has a short "lifetime" when deep-frozen, since – like other oily baits – it softens quickly. So it must be checked and moved often.

Herring bait is served whole (with or without the head), in half-pieces, in bits, or in filet form. The cut variety, divested of its head and breast fins, is a classic salmon bait along the

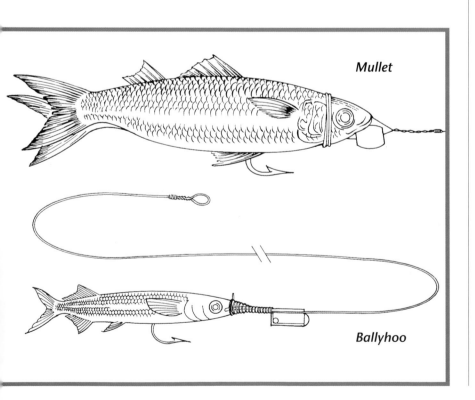

Mullet

Ballyhoo

Herring

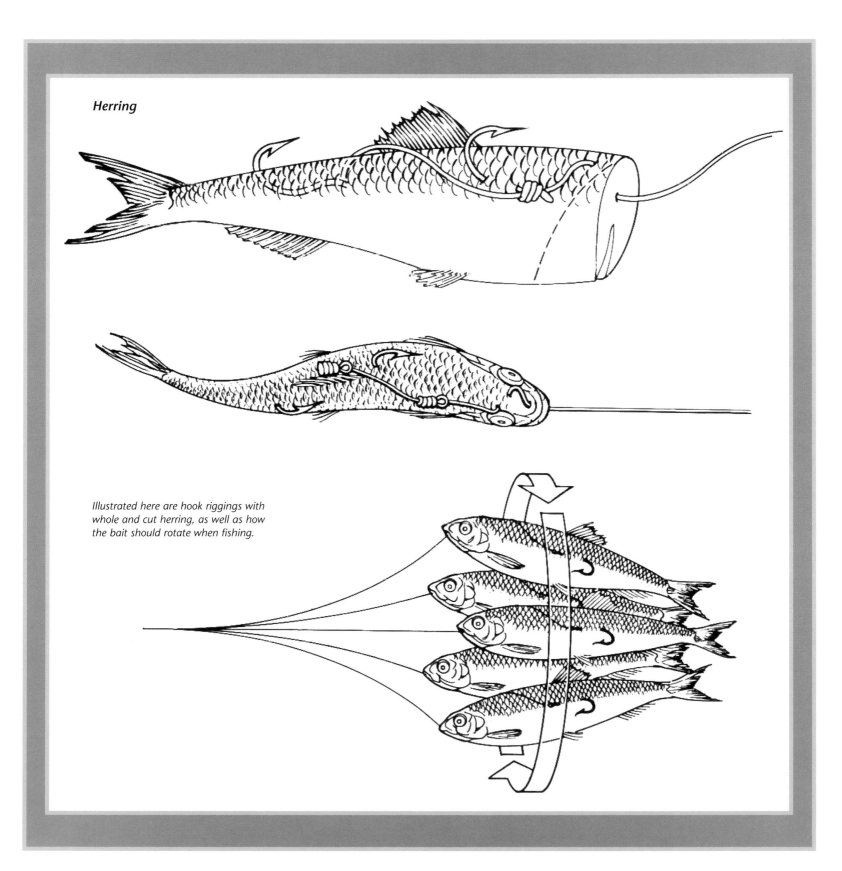

Illustrated here are hook riggings with whole and cut herring, as well as how the bait should rotate when fishing.

western coast of North America. Opinions about how to cut and rig it, however, are numerous. If the cut is straight, the herring will rotate in wider and slower movements than if it is cut at, say, 45 degrees. Most of us prefer a rapid rotation, but it should not be trolled faster than 2.5 knots.

The best hook arrangement is a double one, with the upper hook placed closest to the cut, passing from the inside outward. The other hook is hidden in the tail spool.

Squids

Octopi, squids and cuttlefish occur pelagically in large schools, and make superb bait. These " soft cakes" are gobbled unhesitatingly by fish, and they hold the hook well even with no drop-back.

A squidd is best trolled close to the boat. Rig it carefully so that the bait is balanced: it should not slide on the hook or divide itself. Time is needed to sew up such a bait, so try to do several at the same time. Squids can be kept frozen for long; if thawed and put in plastic bags, they keep for 3-4 days on ice. But never lay the bag directly on ice; place something like sailcloth in between. This is because a squid loses color and becomes untasty if it comes near fresh water. So it must be thawed in salt water.

Worms

The nightcrawler is probably the world's commonest freshwater bait, an all-rounder that helps the troller mainly to catch walleye, bass, perch and char. The worm is usually put on the hook behind a flashing attractor or artificial lure. Choose the hook size according to the worm's size and the type of predator. If worms are kept dark, cool, and in damp earth, they act much livelier on the hook.

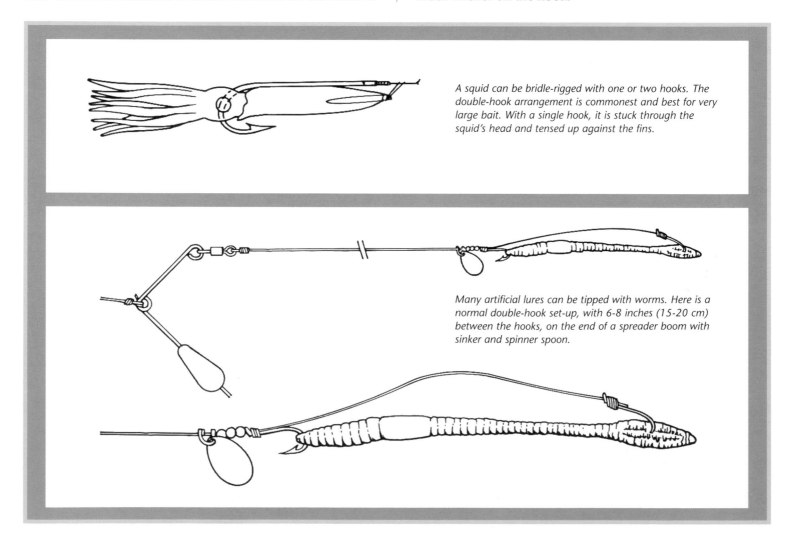

A squid can be bridle-rigged with one or two hooks. The double-hook arrangement is commonest and best for very large bait. With a single hook, it is stuck through the squid's head and tensed up against the fins.

Many artificial lures can be tipped with worms. Here is a normal double-hook set-up, with 6-8 inches (15-20 cm) between the hooks, on the end of a spreader boom with sinker and spinner spoon.

Terminal tackle

For most trollers, the leader is an essential part of the equipment. It is what always takes the worst knocks, and the greatest responsibility in the final stage of the fight. Scraping against the boat keel, railing, and possibly hard-skinned fish bodies, are things it has to tolerate. Then it should be strong and flexible enough to survive hard jerks and fast jumps. A good leader is also easy to grip, and to guide toward the gaff or landing net.

Initially a leader must succeed in presenting the bait attractively, so that it releases the fish's striking instinct. Without a leader, you cannot get very far, no matter how much other gear you have.

Trolling leaders are mostly tapered and divided in several sections, which may be of different materials. Between these, we tend to place a swivel or sinker, shock-absorber or diving planer. Bait moves best on the end of a long limp leader, rather than of a short stiff one. This is especially true when fishing with a metal line, diving planer, or heavy sinker. A limp leader is also better at taking the zest of a big striking fish.

Big-game fishermen generally follow the IGFA rules for composing leaders. The IGFA accepts a leader length of 15 ft (4.57 m) in saltwater line classes up to 20 lbs (10 kg), and a length of 30 ft (9.14 m) above that. In fresh water, though, the leader must not be longer than 6 ft (1.82 m). But the IGFA allows a reel line to be doubled a certain number of times above the leader. The combined length of double line and leader must not, in salt water, exceed 20 ft (6.1 m) in line classes up to 20 lbs (10 kg), or 40 ft (12.19 m) above this. In fresh water, it must not go over 10 ft (3.04 m). Moreover, according to the IGFA, only when the leader reaches the rod tip should anyone grab the leader to guide the fish within reach of a gaff or net.

Ever more leaders are made today with an eye to catch-and-release fishing. The baited hook then sits on a short wire leader, which is coupled by a swivel or spiral link to the rest of the leader. When the fish is brought alongside the boat, judged as to size, and possibly marked, it is set free at the swivel. Sometimes the wire is cut next to the hook.

Leader materials

The fish species and fishing place determine what material the leader should be made of. But there is a trend toward ever more use of monofilament line. Leaders also vary in dimensions, meaning strength and diameter. Besides monoline, they are made of single- or multistrand wire, which may nylon-coated. Monolines and wire come in breaking strengths of over 400 lbs (180 kg). Some are dark-hued to give better camouflage.

In the future, leaders of fluorocarbon and titanium will certainly come to overshadow these older materials. Fluorocarbon is almost invisible in the water, absorbs very little and makes strong knots. Titanium wire comes in single or multiple strands and is rust free. It does not kink, is soft and light, and can be knotted or joined to wire. Final advantages are its negligible stretch and small diameter in relation to its strength.

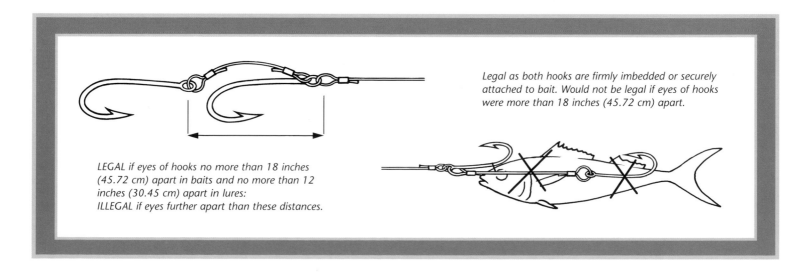

LEGAL if eyes of hooks no more than 18 inches (45.72 cm) apart in baits and no more than 12 inches (30.45 cm) apart in lures:
ILLEGAL if eyes further apart than these distances.

Legal as both hooks are firmly imbedded or securely attached to bait. Would not be legal if eyes of hooks were more than 18 inches (45.72 cm) apart.

Among other components of a leader are the hook, swivel, snap, and sleeve. The wire is coupled with special pliers, or tied by hand. Well-stocked shops sell ready-mounted trolling leaders for different purposes.

On multistrand wire, as well as thick monoline, coupling loops are added all around with the help of sleeves. It is also usually a sleeve that connects the leader and hook. There are various models, sizes and qualities of sleeves – for instance, for wire and/or monoline. Crimping tools exist with cups for sleeves of different size numbers. These are extremely effective, as long as the wire or mono-line has been laid correctly in the sleeve – that is, parallel and not crosswise. Never squeeze the ends of sleeves, and remember that sharp edges may soon ruin the wire.

Hooks

A perfect all-round hook is a fantasy; instead we match the hook size to the dimensions of the bait and the fish, as well as to the rod, reel and line. It is impossible to run a strong hook into a large fish's mouth with light equipment.

The circle hook is receiving increased attention on diverse trolling fronts; particularly solid during the fight for the fisherman, it is merciful for the fish. It comes in different models, and there are even hybrids of the ordinary J-hook and circle-hook. The circle hook almost always catches in the angle of the fish's jaw, holds its grip well, yet is still easy to remove from the fish's mouth.

Big-game fishermen use forged, flattened, short-shanked hooks. They speak of two variants, one with a straight barb, and one whose barb is angled – kirbed or reversed - to the hook shaft. Mustad Southern Tuna is a popular straight model, and Mustad Sea Master is an equally famous angled version. The straight type is common in big-game fishing with both artificial and natural baits, particularly when trolling for long distances with a live bridle-rigged bait.

For salmon bait of the cut kind, hooks like Siwash are the rule. Round-beaten, short-shafted, but long-tipped and angled, they are strong and penetrate well, tending to sit securely even during the wildest fights. Straight Siwash single hooks are popular on the very lightest flutterspoons.

Nickel- and tin-plated hooks easily lose their sting, since they rust. Keep such a hook clean of oxides; always check that it is sharp, and that the hook eye is intact. The latter can otherwise harm the wire or monoline.

Rechargeable, battery-driven hook-sharpeners greatly speed up the job, and can deal with a wide range of hooks, usually giving better results too.

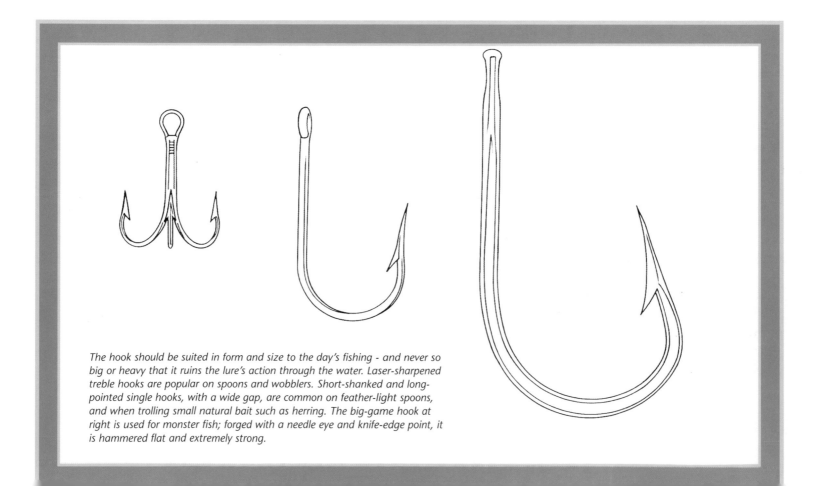

The hook should be suited in form and size to the day's fishing - and never so big or heavy that it ruins the lure's action through the water. Laser-sharpened treble hooks are popular on spoons and wobblers. Short-shanked and long-pointed single hooks, with a wide gap, are common on feather-light spoons, and when trolling small natural bait such as herring. The big-game hook at right is used for monster fish; forged with a needle eye and knife-edge point, it is hammered flat and extremely strong.

Swivels

The chief task of a swivel is to rotate and counteract line twisting. Naturally it should also help the lure to move like a fish as much as possible. Therefore, adapting the swivel's size to the line dimension and other equipment is important. If you have several swivels on a leader, they should be of the same type, material and size. Smaller swivels rotate easier than larger ones.

A leader with a sinker, flashing attractor, and lure requires at least three swivels: one in front of the sinker to eliminate line twisting, and the other two on both sides of the attractor to prevent leader twisting.

Many people use a swivel with a snap as the connecting to the lure. But this is usually needless, if the terminal tackle is effectively attached to the reel line. In ordinary trolling, the lure generally moves better with a snap alone – and best of all with a loop knot.

The swivel's rings often reveal its quality. Sloppily soldered rings, for example, can damage the line and make it break at a knot. Preferable swivels are the ones with stainless-steel, solid rings. A ball-bearing swivel rotates best if the reel line is tied to the ring on the swivel's pin.

Trollers frequently use three-way swivels when the reel line, lure line, and sinker line are attached by three different knots. Tests have shown that the most effective three-way swivel is a self-made one. Place three swivels in a large loop ring; one swivel may be provided with a snap. Since the swivels can run freely in the ring, they center themselves and do not put too much pressure on any single swivel eye.

Snaps and links

Among swivels with snaps, we find several types with different kinds of locking mechanisms. In general, American proprietary snaps, with or without ball-bearing swivels, are preferable. The snap's strength is determined by the wire's thickness and hardness, while its security depends on how well it locks.

In the world's big-game arenas, a double ring Coastlock snap swivel, where the snap is connected to a second ring, rather than the swivel stem, is usually considered unbeatable. The extra ring prevents the snap from rising and locking itself during the outward run. Sampo's McMahon snap, and the corkscrew snap, have many adherents. The latter type is strong, easy to work with, and impossible to open by mistake.

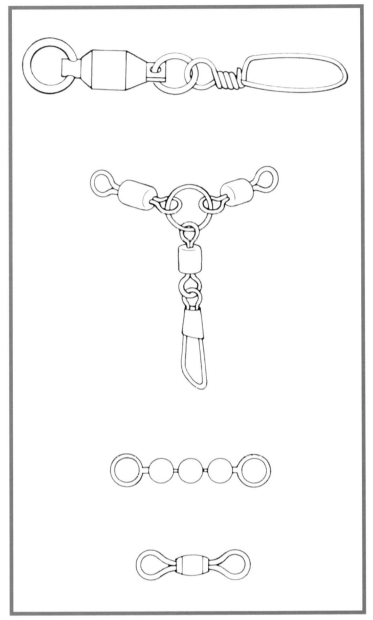

Types of swivels. At top is a big-game ball-bearing swivel, with two solid rings and a coastlock hook. This is the king of them all, and comes in various sizes. The self-centering three-way swivel was built by the author from a ring and three swivels, one of these being a snap swivel. It is worth noting that a solid ring, constructed with no overlaps, is far stronger than a feather ring of the same dimensions.

The bead-chain swivel is a favorite of trollers, due to its supple and flexible form - plus its reliability, which is partly a result of distributing the load on the swivel over many joints.

A barrel swivel of split-head type is better in several respects than one with a single head or twisted eye.

However, I have seen leaders get snarled in the " corkscrew" and snapped by wild salmon leaps. This catch is also conspicuous – for better or worse – because its structure draws a lot of water after it.

Other kinds of links, more or less commonly found in the end tackle, are the duolock snap, the bead.chain swivel, the butterfly link and the glide link. Handy and quickly coupled, they come in different materials, strengths and sizes.

The ring, too, is a type of coupling arrangement, which you should choose with great thought and make special demands upon. The split ring and the solid ring are two versions. Their reliability depends on their strength, resistance to corrosion, and locking arrangement. The solid ring use to be the best. In size, they should be suited to the given lure and hook. With several rings between the lure and hook, one can hook the fish better and ensure that, if it jumps, no break will occur between the lure and hook

Personal equipment

How should a well-dressed trolling fishermen make sure he is protected from head to toe? The answer obviously varies with the latitude, the coast, the season and so on. What can be an advantage on the open sea, such as being easily visible, may prove a great drawback in smaller waters.

Some kind of life-vest, life-jacket or survival suit is obligatory, of course. I never sail south without a Florida cap, Polaroid sunglasses, and antisolar cream. My clothes always include a long-sleeved cotton shirt to shade my arms, and a pair of long light pants with a couple of zippers that can turn them quickly into shorts.

Shoes or boots should be strong, water-repellent and well-sewn, with non-slip soles, so that you can move securely and dry-shod on board. Boots are definitely more protective, but seldom as comfortable.

On your head, according to the climate, there may be a visor, a fishing cap made of Gore-Tex, a knitted cap or a balaclava. In addition there should always be a pair of finger-gloves onboard.

Right: A small boat has many advantages and, with functional equipment, can be turned into an efficient trolling machine.

It is easy to transport between waters, enabling the fisherman to experience a varied sport in diverse surroundings. Often it is shallow-going, whicch permits fishing in waters that are inaccessible to a large, deep-running craft.

Boats and their fittings

For most sportfishermen, a boat is just a way of getting to and from fishing spots. But a boat means a lot more than that to a troller. It is an instrument for fishing, every bit as important to his or her equipment as a rod, line and reel.

A trolling boat may be anything from a small, flat-bottomed car-roof vessel to a big, deep, V-shaped motor cruiser driven by hundreds of horsepower. How the boat looks will depend on when, where and how you fish, and naturally on the size of your pocketbook.

Modern trolling gear has made it possible to fight fish all the time from the ice-melt to the icing-up, and no matter whether they swim deep or shallow. Consequently, the ideal trolling boat should be designed as much for sunny summer days as for chilly winter days. In other words: seaworthy, durable, and

Right: A big boat renders trolling less dependent on the weather and waves. It also off better protection, and room for both fishing and boating equipment. Comfort and sp on board usually mean that you can stay longer at the fishing sp

functionally fitted out. But a perfect trolling boat, suited to all types of water, is and will probably remain a fantasy.

When it comes to trolling boats for private use, most of us select from open center-console boats, walk-around boats and cabin boats in the classes 17-25 feet (5.2-7.6 meters). Here the chances are best of finding an all-round boat that can be transported from one kind of fishing environment to another, while letting you fish shallow inshore waters as well as the deep waters beyond.

The rapid spread of big-game fishing on the world's seas, for top-ranking sportfish such as tuna and marlin, has also led ever more boat manufacturers to make comfortable trolling versions of their flagships in the classes of 30-60 ft (9.1-18.2 m). It is among these flybridge models that we usually encounter the best-known charter boats.

Choosing a trolling boat

When you buy a boat, it is essential to be guided by reality, not personal dreams. A first-time purchaser should analyze his or her requirements very carefully. Try to decide what conditions the fishing will mostly be done under, within the foreseeable future, and base your selection on them. Then you will be most likely to fish both enjoyably and fruitfully.

The foremost rule is that a fishing boat must be as safe as possible. To this end, collect a maximum of facts about the type of boat in question. Many trollers use their boats more during seasons of bad weather than in periods of fine weather, since the fishing is best at the former times. Make sure that the railings or gunwale all round the boat provide support above your knees. The grab-rails should also be strategically placed so that you can move about easily and safely on board.

Check, too, that the scarn deck is wide and strong enough for all the desired equipment to be mounted.

Regardless of what material a boat is made of, it needs maintenance. Some parts are more exposed to wear than others on a trolling boat. The best place to put equipment is not as obvious on a big boat as on a little one. You should see to it that the electronics, for instance, can tolerate salt water and spray. Regularly inspect the steering and engine controls, fittings and hull, stern equipment and the engine itself.

For most sportfishermen, a boat purchase often ends with some sort of compromise. A good first-time buy can be a well-kept boat that has been used by another person who sport-fishes in the same way as you do. Practical and even difficult problems of installation and fitting will then have been solved already.

The boat's size

In a center-console boat, either big or small, you can move freely from the stem to the stern, and from side to side. Thus, fishing and fighting the fish can be done very effectively from this type of boat. In practice, the fishing space may also be more extensive on a small boat than on a much longer and wider one.

Generally speaking, the same advantages – together with significantly better weather protection and stowage space – are found in a walk-around boat. As the name indicates, the cabin is surrounded by a broad sunken passage. Many trolling fishermen in both the New and Old Worlds consider this boat type as close to the ideal as one can come, for fishing on large inland waters and along open coasts.

Small boats tend to allow fishing in shallower water than do the bigger, deep-going types. In addition, fish are not as shy of a small boat. The size and weight are also decisive for whether a boat can be transported by trailer, for easy movement from one body of water to another.

The limits of a little boat are clearest in terms of space for equipment – or if you fish on the open sea. Out there, they provide minimal shelter from wind, rain and breaking waves. Personally, though, I do not think this is such a bother, compared with the mobility of a small boat. But it does become troublesome when trolling equipment cannot be constantly kept in place on the boat. Storage space in a small boat is neither secure nor extensive enough. It is then essential, from the outset, to plan and put away the equipment in the right way,

so that the work of carrying things is minimized and will not diminish your enjoyment or time.

As a rule, in my experience of fishing on small boats, a motor-driven boat should always be driven from a console. Unfortunately, many consoles are far too small for the equipment which a trolling fisherman wants to have available and keep in view.

Larger, decked boats have the great advantage of giving good protection from wind and rain – and, in a wider perspective, of being usable on rough open waters. Their roominess offers not only the opportunity of overnight sleeping, but also easy positioning and handling of trophy catches and equipment, such as a communications radio, echo-sounder, navigation instruments, downriggers, outriggers, fighting chair, lures, tackle, and personal belongings. Besides, their comfort and safety can be much better. These benefits, which enable one to get the most out of the boat, have led many fishermen to invest in a large craft and a permanent place in the harbor.

The helmsman's area

Good elbow room should be the hallmark of the cockpit, no matter whether you wear shorts or a survival suit. The steering gear, engine controls, and other instruments should be well-placed, protected, easily accessible and visible, without blocking your lines of sight.

The range of instruments has naturally influenced the whole center console and the cabin panels. Some modern center consoles can be folded forward, giving easy access to the deck and to any fuel space or equipment underneath them. The console should ideally be protected against wind and rain from three directions by a plexiglas windshield– ample enough to shield both the instruments and the helmsman.

Moreover, a strong rail should run around the steering unit. It may be extended into a T-top or a spray hood, which gives further protection against sun and rain from above.

Rig equipment

The importance and function of a side deck on a trolling boat are often neglected. Most of the praise or blame fall upon the hull design, cabin and engine. Yet the boat's gunwale is what has to take the first, and sometimes worst, knocks when it comes to protecting your boat, your life, and your gear. The top side and rails should be high enough to give support, at least up to the knees, for a medium-tall adult all round the boat.

If the rod-holders and rig equipment are properly positioned, even a small deck space allows you to cover considerable width and depth at the boat's sides and astern.

To a trolling fisherman, the railing – in terms of the scarn deck – also provides an extremely important platform for fishing, both downward and sideways. This is where everything from single rod-holders to complete downriggers and outrigger poles is attached.

The scarn deck on a trolling boat has to be wide and strong, as well as made of a material that is tough, durable, and easy to work. Top-quality wood of correct dimensions is a superb side deck material. If, for example, you add a fiberglass mounting for a downrigger, you will normally need to strengthen it from below with marine plywood.

Rod-holders

For many of us, the first rod-holder is a mobile type that can be attached to a railing. Its steadiness, and ability to point the rod in desired directions, are important Moreover, it must allow you to quickly remove the rod, in order to make a hookup or move to a fishing chair.

A rod-holder's size and strength should be suited for the fishing in question. It would be foolish to put, for example, big-game equipment in simple plastic holders. Such equipment demands robust metal holders with replaceable linings – whether they are flush mounted into side or stern deck, in fighting chairs, or in the rod launcher of a leaning post. Many rod-holders have a cross-pin in the bottom that fits into the gimbal butt of the rod handle, keeping the rod in a definite position. It also prevents the reel from knocking and chafing against the rod-holder's upper edge. In any case, when moving at speed or on rough waters, it can be smart to secure the rod set-up with safety ropes.

Remember to locate the rod-holders on board in a pattern so that they spread the trolling lines as much as possible and avoid tangles. Make sure, too, that they are within reach and can be surveyed from the driver's seat. A rear-view mirror helps the solitary troller to see aft.

Downriggers

A downrigger has the advantage of being able to bring even a leaf-thin lure down to a depth of hundred meter, by means of a sinker weight and line release. When the fish strikes, it pulls line from the release, and can be played directly with the ordinary fishing gear.

Thus, a downrigger is an independent part of the equipment, consisting of an arm with a roller guide and a spool of wire line that runs through the guide. On the wire's end is a heavy sinker weight, in a snap swivel. Also on the wire, or attached to the sinker, is a line release.

Most downriggers have a drag system, depth counter, and rodholder as well. But not all downriggers, or their components, can tolerate salt water – and this is something to watch out for.

The wire's length and strength may vary a little with the rig's size, but around 200 ft 60 m) and 130 lbs (60 kg) test strength are common. The sinker usually weighs 3.5-15 lbs (1.5-7 kg).

Downrigger arms come in short or long sizes of 1-6 ft (30-180 cm), or may be telescoping. The arm length depends on how you want to locate your rigs on board, whether you need to keep the line clear of the propellers and engine mounting, how easy it is to take the sinker weight in and out, and so forth. The sinker is moved either manually or with a small electric motor.

To reduce the stress on the wire, arm and other components, the downrigger should be started and stopped softly. It is also helpful if the rig can be operated with one hand – for letting down, retrieving, and stopping. Adjust the drag so that it slips lightly during the descent, or if the weight gets snagged on the bottom. You should be able to retrieve manually even with an electric rig, in case the current is cut off.

The rig's tip roller should be swiveling and automatically tracks the downrigger weight toward the depths. The pulley itself should be sufficiently deep or protected to prevent the wire from sliding out. Finally, never load the spool with longer or thicker wire than what is specified by the rig manufacturer. Obey the instructions as regards the sinker weight, and always have spare parts on board – such as wire, sleeves, weight snaps, and extra sinkers.

A downrigger strains the side or stern deck hard, no matter what type of mounting is used. There are many versions and models of downrigger mountings, but I personally prefer a swivel base. This makes it possible to tackle lures very near the boat, then swing out and lock the arm in the desired direction.

Another common alternative is to mount downriggers on a "trolling bar disk" at the stern. The bar is fixed, at the desired height, in pedestals which are mounted in the stern deck. There are also mounting board which, like the roof-rack on a car, are mounted across the boat. If the bar has the form of an aluminum rail, the rigs can be positioned easily.

When flush mounted rod-holders are fixed to the side decks, the downriggers can suitably be mounted on an adapter with a tubular foot and guide sloe. Slide the foot into a rod-holder, where a cross-pin in its bottom locks the rig in position. A swivel base on the adapter will further increase the choices for positioning. With the rig in an adapter base, you can also quickly lift it away from the side deck when you need swinging room, or when you want to use the boat for other kinds of fishing.

An accessory that can be very useful on long-armed rigs con-sists of a pulley on a piece of cord which is attached to the wire. Popularly called a retriever, it helps to pull in the wire when retackling. The cord can then be fixed in a cleat on the downrigger.

On most downriggers of medium or large size, it is now possible to mount one or more rod-holders. Single-rod holders are usually placed on the rig housing, but double-rod holders generally sit farthest down on the arm. You should be able to angle the holders separately, not least in order to spread out the rods.

Makers of downriggers are relying ever more on computers. For instance, the lure and sinker can be raised and lowered at different speeds through the water. This may be important when you have to get the gear up fast after a big fish strikes. The sinker can also be stopped automatically at the water surface, to reduce the load on the arm and wire. The rig's computer can be programmed so that the lure searches certain depths at various time intervals – an advantage when fishing in and around the thermocline. You can even get the bait to continually follow the bottom contours, at a particular distance so that the sinker does not get snagged.

The smallest and simplest downriggers weigh only a few pounds, and have a low profile to occupy minimal space in a fishing bag. They usually hold 80-100 ft (25-30 m) of wire, have a less sophisticated drag than on larger models, and can be loaded with up to some 5 lbs (2 kg) of sinker weight. The arm length is 12-16 in (30-40 cm). These versions come with or without a depth counter, and can be placed in rowlock holes or clamped to the railing. Despite their modest size, they increase the fisherman's range enormously.

In general, it is the boat's size and railings, side and stern deck – as well as the kind of fishing water – that determine the size, number, and positioning of downriggers. But keep in mind the following:

- place downriggers so that they are not a safety risk on board;
- place them in the rear third of the boat;
- place them so that you can get between them to net or gaff the fish;
- if possible, place long-armed rigs at the sides, and short-armed rigs at the stern;
- place rigs and rods within easy reach and view.

Outriggers

As an aid to fishing, the outrigger holder is older than the downrigger. Its main task is to spread the bait lines beyond the boat's wake. Outrigger arms are normally fished at about 45 degrees from the side of the boat. Around Hawaii, however, they are fished in an almost vertical position, at 60-90 degrees, so that the artificial lures will run just under the surface.

Today's arms consist of aluminum, stainless steel or fiberglass, may be either telescopic or screwed together in sections, and are 15-30 ft (4.5-9 m) long. The shaft requires rigging kits, which usually comprises a halyard line about 100 ft (30 m) long, a shock-cord (with a glass ring in one end and a strong ball bearing snap swivel in the other), a pulley, a line release clip, and an eye strap in the boat.

The shortest outriggers are commonest in center-console boats of up to 20 ft (6 m). They are usually placed in flush holders in the scarn deck. A curved butt section makes them easily portable and collapsible for fishing or transport. Long shafts are found mainly on large motor cruisers, where they may be mounted on the cabin's side and/or on a superstructure, such as a tuna tower. These rods are solidly anchored to the boat with four legs, but are very easy to collapse or raise with a control-knob. Still, they should be secured with a safety rope.

The choice of outrigger depends on the size of the bait, as well as on that of the boat. Most frequently the outriggers are installed about amidships, so that the poles bend aft when in trolling positions. Thus, when a fish strikes, the reel lines do not risk landing in the driver's well and possibly getting caught.

The shafts' bending capacity varies with their construction.

Some are stiffened with several metal spindles. Stiff poles fish well even in rough seas. They may carry double halyards lines, and can spread a number of baited lines at the same time. An all-round outrigger has a stiff lower part and a flexible tip which makes up about 25% of the shaft's total length. Even the shortest version can be a great help. It does become easy to overload in bad weather, which makes the lure jump and splash in the surface – fishing poorly as a result. But this can be corrected by positioning the line and release farther down on a stiffer part of the shaft.

The halyard runs through guides on the shaft, and sometimes also through a tip pulley. On this halyard are one or more clips, in which the reel line is clamped. The warping is done either manually or electrically. The halyard is tightened up once the fishing lines and baits have reached the right places and are not in the way.

Planer boards

Another variant of surfacing trolling makes use of a mast and planer boards. The latter, like an outrigger holder, are fished in the open sea to cover waters that are not disturbed by the boat's passage. They are especially handy when a fisherman wants to present baits in shallow water near land, which is unreachable due to the boat's depth.

A planer board may be a traditional otterboard, but is normally designed for its purpose. It can be made of wood, metal,

In fresh and brackish water, most of us widen our fishing with planer boards. These are sent out sideways from a mast with planer lines, to which line releases and rod equipment are coupled.

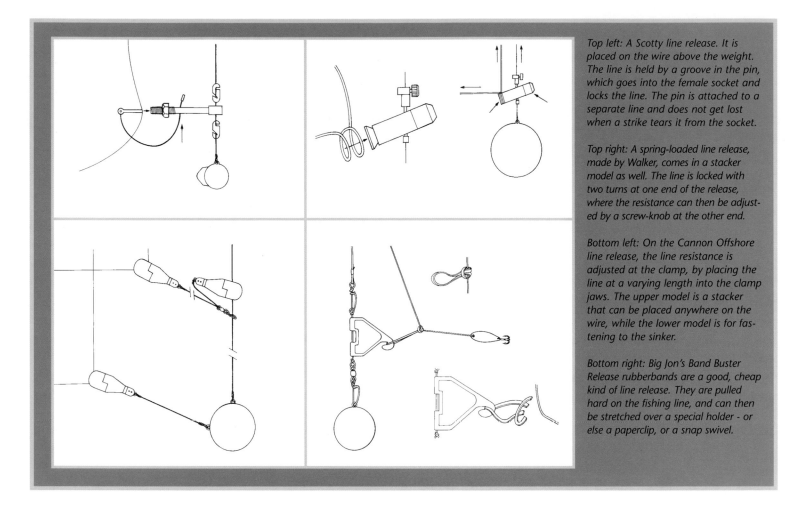

Top left: A Scotty line release. It is placed on the wire above the weight. The line is held by a groove in the pin, which goes into the female socket and locks the line. The pin is attached to a separate line and does not get lost when a strike tears it from the socket.

Top right: A spring-loaded line release, made by Walker, comes in a stacker model as well. The line is locked with two turns at one end of the release, where the resistance can then be adjusted by a screw-knob at the other end.

Bottom left: On the Cannon Offshore line release, the line resistance is adjusted at the clamp, by placing the line at a varying length into the clamp jaws. The upper model is a stacker that can be placed anywhere on the wire, while the lower model is for fastening to the sinker.

Bottom right: Big Jon's Band Buster Release rubberbands are a good, cheap kind of line release. They are pulled hard on the fishing line, and can then be stretched over a special holder - or else a paperclip, or a snap swivel.

styrofoam or glasfiber material. The important point is that it should be simple to use, and ride well on the water. As a rule, the bigger it is, the better it tolerates high speed and rough seas. The yard-long versions are heavy to retrieve, so they put a hard strain on the mast and line spool. To be seen properly, a planer should be painted in some conspicuous color, and carry a pennant or flag.

Between the mast and planer board runs a rope, over a mast pulley that is sometimes spring-loaded. On this line, a release can slide freely. The fishing line is coupled to the release, so that the lure can be presented 80-100 ft (25-30 m) from the boat. If a small diving plane, of the Kuusamo type, is placed between the lure leader and the reel line, you can fish both down and out. When the fish strikes, it pops the line free and can be fought directly from the rod.

The mast, generally 3-6 ft (1-2 m) long, bears one or two line spools that are adjustable in height. It should be made of saltwater-resistant material. Place it as far forward as is practical, and mount it very steadily. Reels with clutch sys-

tem are an advantage. The rope is usually of colorful dacron, about 165 ft (50 m) long, with a test strength of around 130 lbs (60 kg).

Some simple planers, of the Yellow Bird and Rover type, are attached directly on the fishing line and kept in place by a line release. When the fish strikes, the planer slides down the line to a stop, or is just let go. In calm weather, such planers can bring the lure far out to the side, into areas where shy fish may lurk. They take up little room, and are very handy to have in your tackle box.

Line releases

Also called a clip, this device is among the most important in trolling. Its job is to hold the fishing line in place until the fish strikes. Then it has to free the line and, at the same time, give enough resistance to resemble a first counterstrike. An essential requirement is to be able to adjust the resistance that is needed to release the line.

Several models and sizes of line releases exist for fishing

with a planer board, downrigger or outrigger. The sliding type is most common with planer boards, while fixed and movable types are used with the latter rigs. Fixed clips are attached to the weight or on the downrigger wire just above it. But a movable line release, called a "stacker", can be placed at any level on the wire. Thus, two releases on the same wire enable you to "stack", or fish with two rods at different depths from the same downrigger. The main point is that a stacker should be easy to place and release on the wire.

The releasing mechanism varies from one type of clip to another. Some have clamping jaws that simply lock the line. On others, the line has to be wound around a spring device or an arm. Alternatively, the line is locked with a plug. One or two rubberbands can also work well as a link between the sinker/wire and the reel line: the band is torn off when the fish strikes.

On most models, the clip's tension can be adjusted by hand. How hard it should be depends on the given fish species, trolling depth and speed, the sea conditions and the lure's form. But keep in mind that some models which look easy to adjust in a shop may be hard to handle when you are out on a swaying boat deck with wet fingers.

Tension setting is crucial

No matter where the release is placed, you have to watch out that the fishing line does not slip in the release: if it does, a big bow will arise in the line between the rod tip and the release. Then the fish will take slack line just after striking and may be hooked badly. At worst, the lure may slide all the way up to the release, get caught in it, and do no fishing whatever. This is best avoided by using, for instance, specially designed downrigger rods in combination with adjustable clips. The soft tip of such a rod bends attentively into tension, right towards the release, so it causes nothing like the pull on the line and clips that an ordinary spinning rod in the same position creates. The deeper you fish, the more obvious this becomes.

To put things simply, the pressure in the release grows with the fishing depth and the length of fishing line that is out. Couple the heaviest equipment (heaviest line, biggest lure) to the release that is farthest down. In general, fish are hooked best on a short line length, and without too little tension. Excessive tension can make it impossible for a biting fish to jerk the line from the release.

It is particularly difficult, and therefore important, to find the right tension when you are fishing at great depths with live bait and big-game equipment in your rod-holder. The fish should feel minimal resistance from the bait when striking – otherwise they may instantly spit out the bait. By tensing up with a bit of curve in the line, having a long line out at 30-65 ft (10-20 m), fine-tuning the clip tension, and trolling slowly, you get the desired "dropback" effect.

The tension in the release can be checked in different ways. Most commonly, one tries from the boat to jerk line with the rod from the release when it is at a normal depth or distance. If the line does not loosen, the resistance is usually too hard. A more reliable procedure, especially when fishing at great depths or for big game, is to determine resistance by using a scale. Tie one end of the fishing line to a spring-scale, then place the line correctly in the release, and clamp it with varying strength. On the scale you can read the weight figures that are needed to pull out the line, at each level of tension and length of line.

Fishing at depth

Rubberbands are very popular as line releases. They are cheap, easy to position, and usable either as stackers or fixed releases. In sizes 12-16, they break with a load of 2-9 lbs (1-4 kg), which is enough for ordinary downrigger fishing for salmon, among other things. Size 32 is used by many who fish with equipment in the IGFA classes of 20-30 lbs (10-15 kg). Those who hope to hook a seagoing express train on gear of 50-130 lbs use No. 64 rubberbands. The disadvantage of a rubberband is that its resistance cannot be adjusted, but a solution is to join several of them together. They also have a very short lifetime, being quite sensitive to sunlight. So they should always be stored as cool and dark as possible.

A rubberband release is tightened around the fishing line to prevent it from slipping through, and is coupled to a snap of the Elasti-Clip variety, or to a plain paperclip. This in turn is attached to the sinker or wire. The rubberband is pulled off when the fish strikes. Pieces of it may stay on the line, but usually pass through the rod guides and level-wind. However, get them off as soon as possible.

The "clothespin" model is an easy-to-use version. Its components are tension pads clamp, nylon-covered wire, and a snap swivel that attaches to the sinker. Its tension is adjusted by placing the fishing line more or less far into its jaws. It is available with variable pinching power in the jaws.

Wire and sleeves are parts in the line release that should be carefully checked, because breaks can easily occur here and result in corrosion. Exchange the wire for a terylene line. Moreover, rubber pads in the clamping jaws may stick together when a line release stays out of use for long, and this is avoidable by putting a piece of tinfoil between the jaws. As the pads wear down in time, the clamping strength weakens.

On other release clips, the line release mechanism consists of a powerful C-shaped wire arm. This kind of clip creates very little wear on the line and is particularly appreciated by those trolling with superlines or in a saltwater milieu. The line goes around the arm in a loop after having first been twisted 5 to 10 turns. The arm's tension is then adjusted with a screw or slide. When the fish strikes, the C-arm open and the line is released.

Fishing at the surface

Planer-board releases should be easy to mount and run on the planer board rope. They generally consist of a metal device, like a ring or paperclip, which has pinch pads. The tension is adjusted by placing the fishing line at different distances into the clips. A fast-wiggling plug needs harder pressure than a light spoon. After the strike, the release slides down along the planer board rope, so you should have a bunch of clips available for continuous fishing.

The range of clips for outriggers is much wider than for planers. Here you can find everything from the simple " clothespin" to the roller-guide version.

Trip-Eze is a spring-loaded version where the line runs over a strong wire arm, which can be loaded with varying resistance. The same is true of Aftco's "Roller-Troller", where the line goes over a roller guide that minimizes the wearing friction. The Roller-Troller can also be obtained as a flatline clip. Its release mechanism is mounted in a nylon-covered wire, on whose other end is a strong snap swivel. This construction enables it to be located at many places on board where you want to have a flatline fishing with a line release. Thus your lines will be less snarled or windblown, and the lure will run better with improved hooking ability. Flatline clips are easy to make with many different models of line releases. The simplest way is to tighten a rubberband around the fishing line and attach it to the reel handle.

Sinkers

Sinkers can be divided into two categories, downrigger and flatline sinkers. In both groups they vary as regards shape, weight, and sometimes even color. A flatline sinker is used mainly to keep the lure at the desired depth, without twisting the line or hampering the lure's movement. It is usually attached between the fishing line and the leader.

To minimize their resistance in the water, most trolling sinkers have a torpedo-like body. Some are also down-weighted or have a keel to stabilize the lure's movement, so that it will be less prone to peculiar twisting or swaying. Moreover, the sinker should have a swivel at each end.

Another type of sinker, often used when trolling with natural bait, resembles a cigar or egg. It is threaded on the leader and placed just in front of the bait, which is thus made to swim like a fish.

Besides the keel sinker, so-called walking type sinkers are used among trollers, especially for fishing slowly along the bottom. This is a Y-shaped construction: one of its arms can

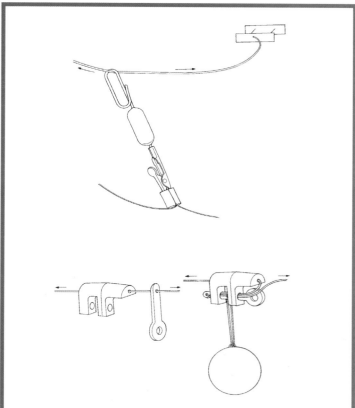

Top: A Laurwick planer-board release. The fishing line, clamped between alligator jaws, is torn loose when the fish strikes. Then the fish can be played directly off the rod, without any resistance from other equipment.

Bottom: A Jettison drop-rig release. This is mounted right on the fishing line, usually 30-50 ft (10-15 m) above the lure. The sinker hangs on a short line stump on a line release pin, and "drops off" when the fish strikes.

take the bumps on the bottom, while the other arm holds the leader and lure away from the bottom.

Downrigger sinkers are in an entirely different weight class, but their size must be suited to the given downrigger. For small rigs that are temporary mount to your boat weights of 3.0-4.5 lbs (1.5-2 kg) are normally used. The very strongest downriggers can take a load of around 16 lbs (7 kg), provided that they are solidly mounted on the boat.

Checking the depth

As long as the sinker is visible in the echo-sounder's conical angle, you can easily keep an eye on exactly what depth it is at. However, the faster and deeper you troll, the larger becomes the difference between the readings on the echo-

sounder and the downrigger. This can be confirmed by eye if you look at the wire's angle to the water surface. What the downrigger's distance counter shows is not how deep you are fishing but how much wire you have out.

There are also tables, produced by the downrigger maker Scotty, which show how deeply different sinker weights run at a speed of 3 knots, with a certain length of line out. These studies used 140-lb test wire and 30-lb (about 0.45 mm) fishing line.

It follows that there are several reasons for having different weights to use at different depths – and, not least, for constantly checking that they are really at the depths where the fish can be found. A normal trolling speed is often 2-4 knots, and it is just in this range, when fishing at depths over 100 ft (30 m), that the changes occur very rapidly.

Illustrated here are a downrigger wire's extension and depth, in feet, for a sinker of 10 lbs (4.5 kg) pulled at a speed of 3 knots, when the line length out is 50, 100 or 200 ft (15, 30 or 60 m). The wire has 140 lbs test strength and a diameter of 0.032 inches (0.81 mm). The faster and deeper you troll, the more weight is needed to keep the sinker in as vertical a position as possible. Try to maintain the wire at an angle of at most 20-30 degrees from the vertical.

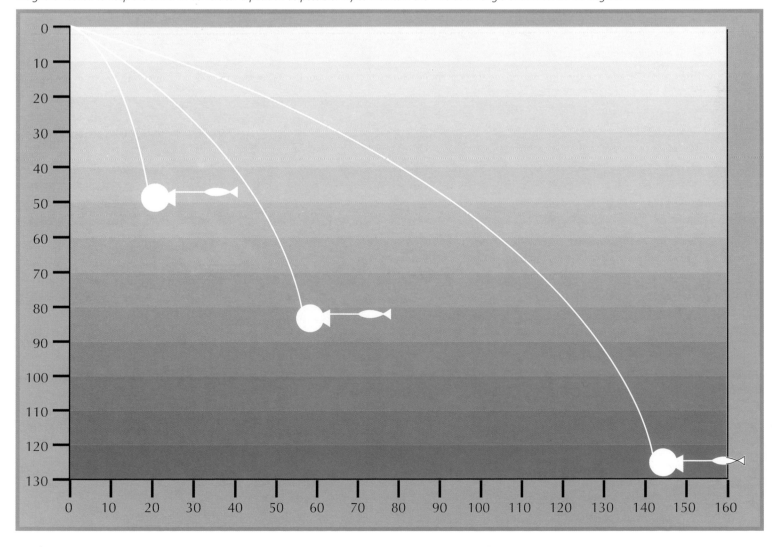

Electronics

Developments in boat electronics have been enormous during the past decade, and to the troller's benefit. All round the world, they are opening up new opportunities. In northern Europe, for instance, the Baltic and many large lakes have become far more accessible than previously. Besides, electronics have made the fishing much safer in both deep and shallow waters. The ability of modern navigation instruments to lead us rapidly and exactly to the fishing places has also reduced fuel costs and increased the actual fishing time. However, high-tech trolling is not what hooks, fights and boards the fish: this calls for a fisherman, not an instrument.

The echo-sounder

An echo-sounder not only gives us an extended "eye" into the world of fish. It is a very important means of rapid and risk-free navigation. Moreover, the information that it supplies about bottom topography, thermoclines, school formations, and individual fish is often stimulating and helps to develop one's fishing.

What we call an echo-sounder is a combination of three units – the monitor, current cable, and transducer. The transducer takes an electrical impulse from the monitor and turns it into a pulse of sound (acoustic pressure) waves. This travels through the water, and is partly reflected back when it hits something – such as the bottom or a fish. Since the speed of sound in water is known (1,460 meters or 4 880 feet per second), the time measured between the outgoing pulse and the incoming echo can be converted into distance. So the echoes from various levels, along with the monitor's image or paper speed, create the picture of the watery world that we see on the screen.

The length of the sound pulses will determine the echosounder's resolution: how close together the fish can be and still appear on the screen as individuals. A short pulse resolves, or separates, the members of a school better than a long pulse. But it is also more sensitive to disturbances, and is not as good for depth-sounding. The latter ability depends on other factors too: the water's condition (such as salinity), the bottom structure, the transducer's conical angle of direction and its mounting, and the wave frequency that it uses. The

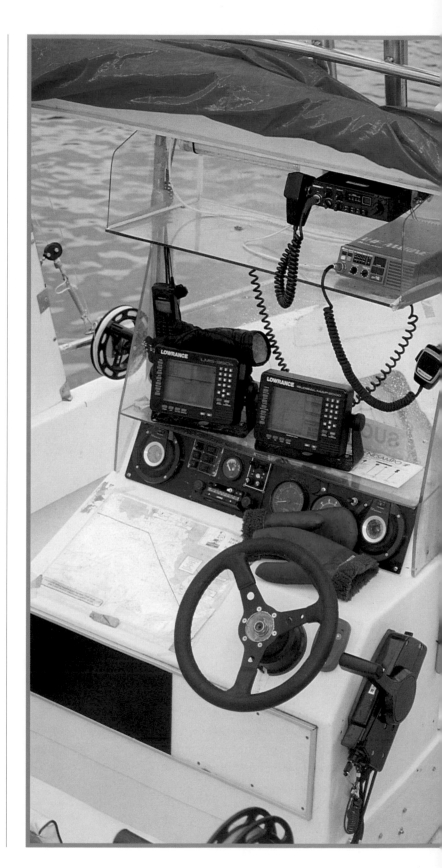

Trolling fishermen are increasingly building up complete electronic navigation systems in their driving environments.

conical angle and the frequency are most important when choosing an echo-sounder for fishing, either inshore or at sea.

Frequency is the number of oscillations per second, commonly measured in kilocycles (kc). A high-frequency echo-sounder is usually said to be one which operates at more than 190 kc, while medium frequency means 75-100 kc and low frequency means 50 kc. Advanced echo-sounders can work with different frequency ranges, which certainly helps to diversify the trolling. For fishing in waters shallower than about 115 ft (35 m), a high-frequency apparatus provides the most information. A low frequency is preferable when fishing at depths of 230 ft (70 m) or more.

The sound waves get weaker as they travel away from the transducer and back again. This loss of strength increases not only with the distance that they travel to an object, but also as their frequency becomes higher. The latter effect is most noticeable in salt water.

Higher frequencies give a clearer echo from small objects, and are less influenced by the motor noise and the hull shape, than lower frequencies. A low-frequency wave, however, is weakened less at long distances. Thus, when it comes to locating fish at great depths, a low frequency is best.

Multidimensional transducers

The transducer sends out sound pulses in a directional pattern that resembles a cone – or more correctly, a lobe. This covers an angle whose size depends on the transducer you use. Such a conical angle might be compared with an adjustable spotlight. The more concentrated the beam is made, the stronger and more revealing is the light inside it. With a wider field of illumination, the beam can expose a bigger area but with a much lower intensity.

There are transducers with conical angles between 5 and 60 degrees. Those with angles up to 15 degrees are regarded as narrow-coned, whereas wide-angle transducers are between 35 and 60 degrees. Normal transducers tend to have a conical angle of 20-30 degrees.

Whatever lies inside the conical angle will reflect sound, and is shown on the monitor as if it were right under the boat – even though, of course, it is not. The wider the angle, the more of the bottom will be exposed. Thus an 8-degree transducer, in the vertical position at a depth of 50 ft (15 m), shows an area of the bottom with a radius of about 6 ft (2 m). This radius will increase in direct proportion to the depth: for example, the same transducer at nearly 200 ft (60 m) exposes a radius of 26 ft (8 m). Yet at the latter depth, a 20-degree

transducer would expose an area some 72 ft (22 m) in radius.

Most trolling fishermen in small boats use 20-degree transducers, which work at high frequencies of 190-200 kc. A wide-angle transducer registers best in shallow water. However, the depth-sounding ability can be improved by working at 50 kc. This combination is preferable if you want to know where the downrigger weights are going.

Multidimensional wide-angle transducers can be pointed in different directions. The monitor can then give us, for instance, a full 60-degree view which covers about 40 meters of the bottom at a depth of 40 meters. Or it might provide three 20-degree pictures, simultaneously visible on separate parts of the screen.

Choosing a fishing sonar

Which type of fishfinder you select depends mainly on when, where and how you fish, as well as on the type of boat. If the fishing water is only in flatland lakes, rivers and coastal zones, with a maximum depth of 165-200 ft (50-60 m), the choice is much easier than if you also fish on deep fjords, vast lakes, or canyon edges out in the ocean. The latter areas call for an echo-sounder of great depth capacity, sensitivity and resolution. To find big fish at enormous depths, a lot of care is necessary with tasks such as installing the transducer and laying the cable.

Among other relevant questions are the following. Should you have a portable echo-sounder or a stationary one? How well-protected should its location be, and how watertight must it be? How much space does it take on the instrument panel? What information about speed, distance of travel, and water temperature does it give? Can it be coupled with a navigator and autopilot? Which echo-sounder is most suited to a given boat and type of fishing?

The LCD sonar

Even though flashers and recorders are still to be seen on instrument panels, it is LCD-sonars that dominate the field these days.

The screen image of an LCD sonar is built up by thousands of liquid crystals, and so the number of "pixels" in the screen is very important for the image's clarity. Often an LCD sonar is easy to handle and can automatically adapt its depth range, picture speed, and sensitivity to the conditions at hand. There are limited possibilities, via replaying, to document what has happened under the water.

Today's LCD sonars provide a clear view of everything from the surface to the bottom. The picture can be in either

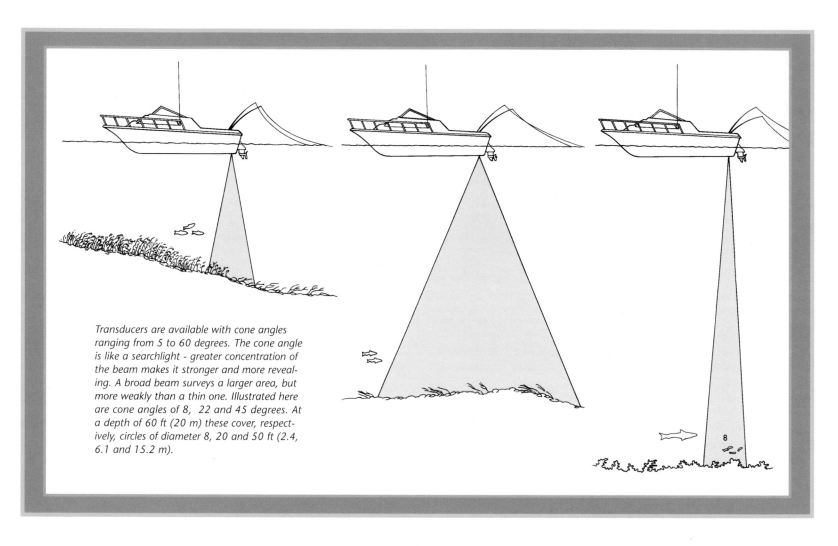

Transducers are available with cone angles ranging from 5 to 60 degrees. The cone angle is like a searchlight - greater concentration of the beam makes it stronger and more revealing. A broad beam surveys a larger area, but more weakly than a thin one. Illustrated here are cone angles of 8, 22 and 45 degrees. At a depth of 60 ft (20 m) these cover, respectively, circles of diameter 8, 20 and 50 ft (2.4, 6.1 and 15.2 m).

black/white or color, or even in three-dimensional form. In the latter case, you get a bottom landscape in perspective – with stones, fish and all the rest.

Many advanced LCD sonars can be bought in small portable models. Their current source is usually a pair of 6-volt batteries. The battery box serves as both a carrier and a steady support in the boat. For those who often use rented boats, a portable sounder is a very handy solution.

Slim, bright and easy to read, LCD sounders with sharp color images of a very high level of image resolution and separation are steadily pushing out the last generation of LCD sounders, which were hard to read in certain light conditions and at certain angles.

The multi-function fishfinder with side-looking sonar is to become ever more common in sportfishing circles. It equips us with an underwater "radar" and reveals the surroundings in a limited vertical or horizontal field under the boat's hull. Its search area can be set to different widths, such as sweeping through a 10-degree field for 330 ft (100 m) in front.

The navigator

For many decades, nautical charts, a compass and an echo-sounder have traditionally been helping most skippers find their fishing spots. The latest, and revolutionary, instrument to guide trolling boats is the navigator. A combined computer and radio receiver, it converts incoming signals to information about position, course and speed, which can be read on a display.

Navigators for sportfishing boats are not fearsome contraptions. What you need, besides the display, are just an antenna unit and electric current. The display can be placed, for example, in a console about half a yard away from the compass and echo-sounder, without risking interference. Being able to

Developments on the electronic side are amazingly rapid. From ever smaller instruments we can extract ever more diverse and useful information, which promotes better and safer fishing. The image screen on this monitor shows information from the speed and temperature sensor, fish finder and navigator. It also plots the boat's course from the starting point until the present position.

mine your position to within less than 3 yards (3 meters).

Navigators are available with different levels of performance and price, so you should approach them with an awareness of your own requirements. In general, a sportfisherman wants to know the boat's position, course and speed. Many of us certainly want a navigator with a brightly lit display, and want it to tolerate tough year-round use in an open boat. Some also want to have the option of coupling other instruments to it, such as an autopilot. The computer's external memory, its ability to be updated and its capacity to store information on waypoints and routes as well as trackplottering are important to investigate when making a purchase.

Even relatively small navigators are convenient and give continuous information on the position, speed and course, as well as data on steering towards various selected "waypoints" on a planned course. They also indicate the strength of radio signals and the battery voltage. Other handy functions are compass correction and "man overboard". The latter means that you need only push a button to record the position, in case of an accident or a place where fish strike.

When the navigator is turned on, it automatically seeks its position without any departure point being programmed in. It gives a signal when this task is done, and it continuously updates the position afterwards, so that you can easily see where you are on a nautical chart – paper or electronic. A plotting function makes navigating significantly easier. Electronic navigational charts exist in a number of advanced versions and packaging (cassettes, CDs) and provide increasingly detailed information of the kind we have expected from traditional charts.

A navigator is very helpful when you want to return to good fishing places – and if you want to feel safe even in darkness, or when the sea-mist closes in fast and cuts off visibility. Like all instruments, though, it can be disturbed or even break down. As long as such things can happen, there are good reasons for preserving your knowledge of traditional navigation techniques.

Radar

In sportfishing waters that are full of islands or boat traffic, radar is becoming ever more common on trolling boats as well. Today's compact radar equipment is absolutely not a luxury, but an extra-safe aid to navigation – not least in darkness and fog.

Radar works like an echo-sounder, but makes use of radio waves instead of sound waves. The waves are reflected when

carry away the navigator when you leave the boat is frequently desired, and there are pocket-sized GPS navigators with plotter functions that can be held in one hand.

For many years, positioning information was provided by the Loran and Decca navigation systems from land-based transmitters with limited range. The reigning system now is GPS (Global Positioning System), which was developed by the United States Defense Department. Employing time-based distance measurements, GPS operates with 21 satellites and three more in reserve. Information is normally taken on board by a 12-channel GPS-receiver.

Systems that improve positional accuracy even more are the American WAAS (Wide Area Augmentation System) and the European EGNOS (European Geostationary Navigation Overlay Service). With a compact antenna that receives DGPS (Differential GPS) and EGNOS/WAAS signals, you can deter-

they hit objects, whose direction and distance are then displayed on a screen. Your own boat is always in the center of the radar image. The boat's position, relative to land and other vessels, is shown continuously. You can also get the radar to produce an alarm if the boat goes on a collision course. Both small and large trolling boats can increase their ability to reflect radio waves by carrying a radar reflector.

Radio and telephone

For today's far-traveling fishermen, it is important to remember that the rules for using communications equipment vary from country to country. What is allowed in your home waters might well be forbidden in neighboring waters. So be sure to check which channels are available for which purposes. In order to be fairly sure of getting radio contact in an emergency situation, you should have a transmitter power of at least 5 watts, and a boat antenna.

The new generation of advanced VHF telephones allows you to make calls anywhere in the world over the telecom network as well as download computer files.

VHF offers coverage everywhere around the clock. This is the system relied upon by most trolling boats of medium to large size. The equipment has become increasingly convenient through the years. Among sportfishermen, the small hand-held versions are popular. A stationary VHF installation, however, generally has a superior range.

A boat with VHF can have its bearings taken and be given radio escort. You can even listen to rescue operations and possibly be able to make a contribution if you are in the vicinity; channel 16 is the international emergency channel. It is also over VHF that coastal radio broadcasts calls, weather forecasts, navigational warnings, and so forth. VHF is without doubt the most secure system, and is now, via DSC (Digital Selective Calling), increasing security even more in emergency situations. Having VHF equipment requires permission.

A good antenna is needed for solid radio contact. In general, the higher the antenna is placed, the longer the range will be. If you have several antennas, make sure that they are spread at different heights, to minimize interference between the instruments on board. Radio equipment also requires excellent "grounding", and the best method is to mount a metal plate on the hull.

A mobile telephone is the most common telecom equipment. By definition portable, it can be used in the boat, in the

The locations of fish are determined largely by the surrounding water temperature. A troller's success depends greatly on his ability to select a boat speed that suits the kind of bait he uses. Information from the depths can be sent up by a torpedo-like transmitter, mounted on the downrigger wire above the weight. Equipped with a blade-wheel and a sensor, it transmits to a monitor where the fisherman can read the data digitally.

car and at home, and it requires no permission. Contact can be made directly or via messages. Its range, however, is limited.

In most places, the traditional CD radio is still the most common communication link between leisure fishing boats. This type of equipment is convenient in size, portable and easy to use. It also has a long range, although it can be sensitive to interference.

Speed and temperature indicators

It is a well-known fact that the water temperature guidelines and sometimes decides where the various fish species occur in lakes, seas, and waterways. To locate the fish, sportfishermen try to check the temperature in different water layers. This can be done most simply by using a glass bottle, a weight, and a removable cork. The most advanced aids are indicators for speed and temperature – together with updated satellite pictures of the fishing area. These are photographs taken with infrared film to reveal the temperature differences in the water, i.e. where warm water meets cooler water.

Some speed and temperature indicators measures both at the surface and at the sinker on the end of a downrigger wire. The current source is the boat's 12-volt battery, and all the information is shown digitally on a little monitor. The other components in the package are a transducer, a cable, and a small torpedo-shaped transmitter. The latter, 9 inches (23 cm) long, has on its bottom a paddle wheel that measures the speed, a sensor, and a wire 12 in (30 cm) long which holds the sinker. This wire has a lower breaking strength than the downrigger wire, which is snapped on the top of the "torpedo". The idea is that, if the sinker gets hung up on the bottom, the light wire will break so that the transmitter can be retrieved.

An indicator is fascinating and instructive to use. Above all, it has proved the profitability of looking for thermal walls, thermoclines, slicks, junctions, inlets. Temperature can change sharply, and surprisingly fast – even in small areas, and in vertical as well as horizontal directions. Speed and temperature indicators are available which measure the light intensity too. With this kind of device, it has been noticed that the light at a depth of 23-26 ft (7-8 m) can become 30% weaker than at the surface when clouds cover the sun, and that 50% of the light can be lost at 50-65 ft (15-20 m).

Temperature charts and thermometers

Temperature charts are divided with a grid system that shows latitude and longitude. Drawn on the map of a lake or coastal area are lots of contour lines, resembling very dense depth curves on a nautical chart. These lines represent temperature variations in the surface water. The areas where many lines run extremely close together are, therefore, hot spots.

As mentioned, there are other and cheaper ways of finding out the water temperature. A common method is to use a hand-held depth thermometer, checking the temperature at different levels from an anchored or drifting boat. In this case the thermometer consists of a cable, 100-200 ft (30-60 m) long, with a sinker and sensor on its end. The cable is run up and down by hand, enabling the temperature to be recorded at various levels, and the depth can be read easily from marks or colors on the cable.

The boat's speed at the surface may not be identical to the lure's speed at a depth of, say, 65 ft (20 m). Down there, quite different conditions can prevail – such as strong currents – which have a negative influence on the lure's motion.

Aids to steering

The autopilot helps you to hold the right course while rigging your fishing lines, as well as to position the boat when the fish is being played, netted or released. In other words, it frees your hands from the wheel. But it does not free your eyes, which have to remain as alert as always.

Autopilots differ in their complexity. Some can be coupled – together with other marine electronics, such as an echosounder and navigator – to a central unit, and can provide automatic navigation from one point to another.

An autopilot consists of several units – for basic functions, supply, steering, and remote control. The steering unit may be needed at both the deck and bridge levels. Mount the autopilot on a stable foundation, since great strain can develop in the steering aid between the wheel or tiller and the motor. The autopilot should also be easy to disengage mechanically.

The compass

A compass is essential on a boat. It shows the way to the fishing places, and can save your life in times of need. There are compasses for all kinds of boats, so buy the best available version for your boat model and fishing environment.

With a bearing compass, you can fix the position of a chosen objective on your nautical chart. Cross-bearings enable you also to determine the boat's position. The compass should be installed with a lot of forethought, so that it is easy to read when navigating, and is mounted upon a steady base exactly on the boat's long axis. Place it as far as possible from iron objects, and from sources of disturbance such as the radio, echo-sounder, navigator and log. Keep in mind the potential errors of a compass, due to natural magnetic deviation and to sources of disturbance, when navigating in large areas of unknown water.

Practical fishing

Matching the fish is a manifolded concept. For many people it refers to the actual fight – how one handles the rod, reel, and net or gaff, when playing the fish. Others take it to mean a whole process: all the way from studying the nautical charts in advance, and the biology of the chosen fish species, to the minute when the boat is moored at the pier after a sporting day.

First you have to pick a location that is right for the season, in other words a part of the environment which – depending on factors such as prey fish, water temperature, salinity and spawning – contains the fish of interest. Examples of seasonal places are deep holes, drop offs, slopes, points, reefs, inlets, estuaries and river junctions. Here you must then select the right "hot spot", which depends on the bottom's structure, consistency and vegetation. Account also has to be taken of the water level, current direction, water clarity, temperature walls, weather, and presence of other fish species or human beings.

The next thing to choose is the right level in the water, a depth where fish exist that are willing to strike. You need to decide on the right tackle, namely what is required besides rod and reel in order to reach the fish at this depth – for instance, a downrigger or a planer board – and at what length of line the lure or bait should follow the boat.

A further step is to select the right lure or bait. You have to choose between spoons, wobblers, plastic lures, attractors and natural bait. Within these families, the right size and color must be decided, to resemble the natural diet of the fish in question as closely as possible – although the color may best be determined by the present visibility in the water. After that, it is important to find the right speed for the boat, giving the lure a movement which will attract the fish to strike.

Finally, the fish have to be fought right, in a way that leaves them unhurted and able to regain their freedom. This means getting everything right when you counter-strike, put pressure on the fish, maneuver the boat, net or gaff the fish, and release it with an optimal chance of survival. The last of these stages in the process are what I want to discuss now.

To begin with, if the fight is to be an enjoyable, exciting game of "give and take", it has to be done with properly dimensioned and balanced gear. The equipment should not be so heavy as to quickly kill both the fish and the fight. There ought to be a good match without denying the fish a safe

A fishing fight's most dramatic moments usually occur as it ends. Coordination on board is then crucial. Here, with the help of a stand-up rod, the fish is brought within reach of the gaffer. The handle's long foregrip enables the fisherman, during the fight, to hold it near the centre of balance and pump rapidly, keeping pressure on the fish. A low-hanging rod belt also allows him to use the power of his hips and legs, not only his arms.

return to its watery element – able to grow, reproduce, and eventually offer somebody a new fight.

For me, this is the essence of sportfishing. It is what I strive for, no matter if I am pole fishing, fly fishing, spinning, jigging or trolling. Whether the fight takes place in a river with my waders on, in a lake with a float-tube around my waist, or in a trolling boat is irrelevant. These equipments are just cosmetics surrounding the fight itself. Nor should there be any need to dress oneself with a boat or a float-tube. Freedom of choice, and being able to accept others' way of fishing, are also key elements of the total perspective of sportfishing.

The strike

Often a fish takes the lure so violently that a strike is unnecessary. The boat's momentum, combined with the resistance when the line is jerked from the release, is usually enough to get the hook well caught in the fish's jaw. The fisherman does not have to think about anything except, perhaps, lifting the rod quickly from the rod-holder to adopt a fighting position – either along the rail or in a fishing chair. But if you are holding the rod in your hand when the fish takes, you should answer with a fast strike. Hard-jawed species such as pike and barracuda may even require two successive strikes.

Sometimes the fish is shy and careful, and gives the lure or bait a close inspection before deciding to take it – or else to swim onward. The striking reflex can be released if the lure speeds up or slows down. So an extra pull on the line, or a couple of turns on the reel or downrigger, may be all the stimulation that is needed. At other times, though, a slowly sinking lure can provide the right inducement.

The fisherman should always have a good view over his equipment. With skill, he can often tell whether the lure's movement is attractive by watching the rod tip – that is, if he cannot see the lure itself. Further important points are that the rod has a short reach, that the reel's drag setting is right, and that you have fast reflexes. It is safest to act as if every strike comes from a record fish.

For big game, hooking and boarding the fish are largely

matters of teamwork, where the fisherman, crew members, skipper and boat must be coordinated efficiently. However, the boat is used differently in various parts of the world, especially in connection with the strike. Some skippers slow the boat down to give the fish a chance to swallow the bait. Others speed up as soon as the slashing bill of the fish has struck the bait and the line has fallen on the water after being jerked from the outrigger's release.

Essential, too, and particularly in big-game fishing, is that you get to know the equipment and the routines on board before you start to fish. You must be aware of how much power the rod gives under pressure, and how the reel's braking system works during the strike and playing (see Chapter 4). You should also be aware of how the terminal tackle is constructed. Most losses of big fish, in fact, are due to the fisherman's inadequate mastery of the equipment.

Playing the fish

Usually a fish rushes away immediately after being hooked. As a rule, this is the longest rush of the whole fight. It may either head into the depths or take place just under the surface. In the latter case, the rush normally finishes with a series of jumps or splashes at the surface.

Let the fish rush, but hold up the rod. If you have a conventional type of rod, keep it at least 45 degrees to the water surface, so that the fish feels the pressure from it. Lighten the drag if it is set hard, or if the fish is big and pulls out a lot of line. For as the spool loses line, the pressure on the line will grow in relation to the preset drag level. When only half the line is left on the spool, twice as strong a pull is needed as at the beginning in order to activate the drag. Thus you should never increase the reel's braking power at this stage. Besides, the more line is pulled out by the fish, the more resistance is caused by the line being pulled

Don't stretch out the landing net toward a fish that is not close enough to the boat. Often the fish will react by expending its last strength on a rush that may go toward the keel or propeller, bringing an undesirable end to the fight. Instead, it should be netted quickly and decisively. Lift it fast and try to close the net bag immediately.

through the water. The very weight of the pulled line is usually just what makes the fish slow down.

It is when the fish stops after the first rush that you have to take command. From then on, you and your equipment must keep the fish moving. Remember not to give the fish any chance of resting, since its ability to regain energy with a pause is much greater than yours.

The commonest method of putting pressure on the fish, and thereby regaining lost line onto the reel, is to "pump" it in. But first the drag should be restored with enough force that pumping becomes possible. Pumping technique depends on the type of rod being used, and on whether you fight the fish from a standing or sitting position.

In any case, the basic idea is to raise and lower the rod smoothly until the fish is brought within reach of the boat. While raising the rod, you take in line; when lowering it, you distribute the line quickly and evenly on the reel. If the fish is large and unruly, you may need a rod belt and a suitable harness in order to hold the rod up, as well as to avoid hurting your body and clothes. With a traditional rod, the fish is pumped home while standing, by working the rod at angles between 45 and 80 degrees to the water surface. Your hands, arms and shoulders are what have to provide the power.

With a stand-up rod, you also use your hips and thighs when playing, and thus minimize the strain on your arms and shoulders. The pumping technique with this type of rod involves short, fast rises and falls, allowing 8-12 inches (20-30 cm) of line to be laid up on the spool at each pump. Such a technique is most effective when the fishing is done vertically and the fish is under the boat, since it then has little chance of turning its head downward to dive abruptly.

From a fighting chair, you pump the fish home by sliding back and forth on the chair, while your legs push against a footrest. You slide backward by stretching your legs, just when a standing fisherman would lift the rod. Once your rod is up, you slide forward by bending your knees, and wind line quickly onto the reel as you lower the rod tip.

On a big-game rod, the model of butt may be important. It is easier to play deep-diving fish with a curved rod butt, and surface-going racers with a straight handle. The curvature usually means that the foregrip and reel stay at a proper working distance from your body. This type also gives a low rod-tip angle, which is an advantage when you want to use the rod's leverage.

Always try to keep a constant pressure on the fish: this is what compels the beast to work against the rod and, in the long run, tire itself out. Never raise the rod so much that you risk creating slack line when the fish rushes toward the boat. Knowing the power bend of your rod will enable you to see, and feel, when it is time to lighten the reel drag. The time has come, at any rate, when the line starts to sing. Never attempt to "break" a fish by putting maximum drag on the reel as you pump in. A soft fish jaw can then easily be ripped apart, and at worst the fish will be lost. The drag should be adjusted so that the fish always has a chance of taking line from the reel if it rushes out unexpectedly.

A fish that jumps with a long line out is seldom able to get free, because of the line pressure. But the risk is much greater when the fish is close to the boat, especially if it has a heavy lure hanging in its mouth. A short, tight, non-stretchy line – combined with the weight and wear of the lure in its mouth – has allowed many a fish to escape near the boat after a long fight.

Try to parry a jump by lowering the rod tip, although not so much that the fish gets slack line. Be sure to lighten the drag when the fish approaches the boat, so that any sudden jerks it makes will not endanger the line. Except in big-game fishing, the line can usually be braked well with your thumb, once the fish is near the boat.

Maneuvering the boat

If you play the fish from a fighting chair, you may need the help of a mate to swing the chair, thus keeping the rod pointed to the place where the line disappears into the water. To assist a tired or inexperienced fisherman in taking home the line, the skipper can back up the boat toward the fish. Another tactic is for the skipper to turn the boat and run parallel with the fish. This enables the fisherman to reduce his drag, and the fish soon tires since it has to pull line in the boat's wake.

In big-game fishing, it is normally necessary to keep the boat and motor going all through the fight. On the other hand, in most cases this is not essential when trolling for salmon. Here you should just try to maintain steering speed until all the tackle is taken in, and then fight the fish from the stationary or drifting boat. But you can operate the motor if you have to move because of the fish, the weather, or other vessels. Thus, stop the motor only when it is time to net the fish – so that the propeller blade will not cut the line and suddenly put an end to the fight. If for any reason you need to keep the boat moving, you will get the most out of the fight by steering around the fish in wide circles.

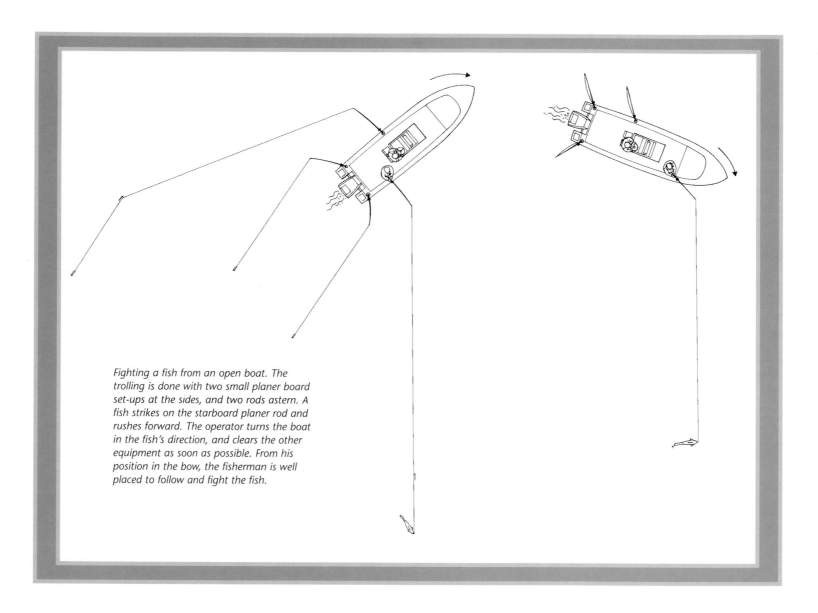

Fighting a fish from an open boat. The trolling is done with two small planer board set-ups at the sides, and two rods astern. A fish strikes on the starboard planer rod and rushes forward. The operator turns the boat in the fish's direction, and clears the other equipment as soon as possible. From his position in the bow, the fisherman is well placed to follow and fight the fish.

One should always be careful not to bring a fish near the boat if it is not yet tired. Its alert jumps, splashes and frightened gyrations are hard to parry, especially if it fights close to the surface. There is then a risk of slack line, and of the fish – with a jump and a hard throw of its head – shaking loose the lure or bait, which may be slung towards the boat. Likewise, there is a good chance of the fish landing on the line and snapping it, or getting tangled in it. Try to keep the fish at a visible distance until the signs of fatigue begin to show: when the rod becomes less strained and the fish's circular movements become ever tighter.

A fish that begins to turn on its side is nearly finished – but not always completely. Often it spends its last strength on a rush just as you extend the landing net or gaff towards it. And with bad luck, it may head straight for the keel or propeller, giving the fight an undesirable conclusion.

Netting and gaffing

Down to the last round in a standing fight, you should maintain a reduced drag, a ready thumb, and a suitable position on board, in order to stick the whole rod into the water if the fish decides to dive under the boat. Do not stretch out the net to try and reach a fish at a doubtful distance from the boat. This will only scare it.

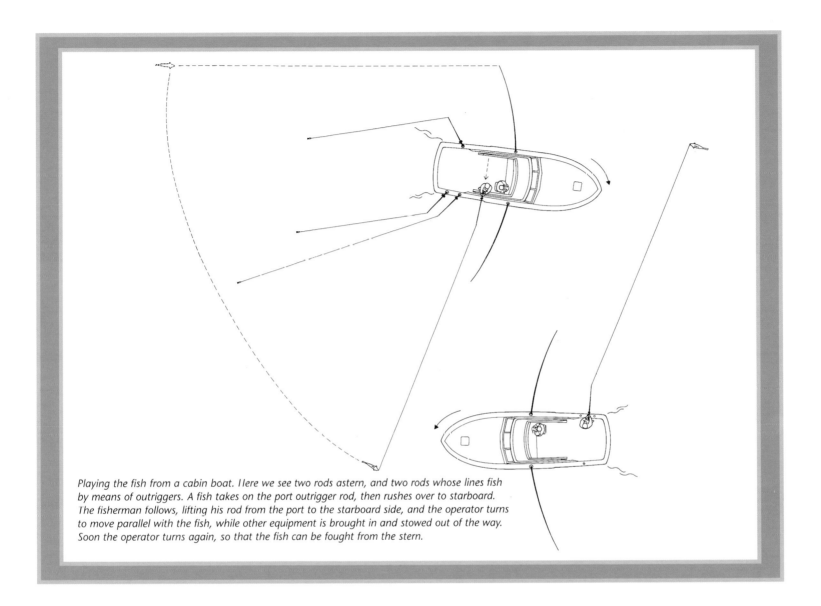

Playing the fish from a cabin boat. Here we see two rods astern, and two rods whose lines fish by means of outriggers. A fish takes on the port outrigger rod, then rushes over to starboard. The fisherman follows, lifting his rod from the port to the starboard side, and the operator turns to move parallel with the fish, while other equipment is brought in and stowed out of the way. Soon the operator turns again, so that the fish can be fought from the stern.

Scoop the fish with speed and determination. The net should be partly under the surface before the fish is pulled in over its frame, head first. Lift the net quickly and try to close it, either by spinning the mesh or by raising it vertically with the shaft along the boat's side. Then shift your hands to the frame and lift it on board. The fish is locked against the side and has little chance of escaping, as long as you have the strength to lift it.

A fish is best gaffed in the head. Ideally the hook can be stuck into the lower jaw, as the fish then stays surprisingly still. It is thus easy to free the fish from the lure with a disgorger and return it unharmed to the water. The hole in its jaw skin is small and will soon heal.

In heavyweight duels from a fighting chair, the last stage is often the most dramatic of all. The skipper must have a good view of everything that happens, so that he can steer the boat quickly. The mate needs room to maneuver the fish alongside the boat. So the fisherman plays a rather passive role during the gaffing, though he has to remain alert. He should stay in the fighting chair with very little drag on the spool, and with the clicker on, so that the fish – if it manages to get loose – will not break the line, or backlashing it on the spool. Any others on board should keep out of the way unless their help is called on.

The climax in big-game fishing approaches when the double line begins to be wound on the spool, and when the ter-

minal tackle's uppermost swivel stays in sight above the water surface. Only when the leader is close enough for a mate's leather-gloved hands should it be grabbed, and the hopefully worn-out fish guided toward the boat side. Do not pull the leader on board: make sure it falls outside, in the water.

If the fish is to be kept, it is first hooked in the head or neck with a flying gaff. Do this while the fish still has its head under the surface – otherwise it may start to roll and thrash uncontrollably in the surface water. Never try to keep a gaffed fish subdued with only your hands; the gaff rope should be quickly lashed on board. Then continue, if necessary, by gaffing in the fish's body before a tail rope is pulled tight at the slender area at the base of the tail. Finally you can knock it for good with a fish billy.

If the fish is to be released, it is sometimes tagged before the leader wire is cut – as close to the hook as possible. Salt water, combined with the fish's stomach acids, will soon dissolve the hook. The fish may need an oxygen supply to its gills before it regains freedom, and is then held with its head down in the water's current direction. Occasionally it is also helped to start off by making slow movements. You can signal to other fishermen that you are marking fish, by raising the IGFA flag with a "T" which stands for tagging.

Salmonoids

The large family of salmonoids is grouped in three subfamilies. One of these includes salmon, trout and char; the other two contain whitefish and grayling.

In the first-mentioned subfamily can be found some of the troller's most pugnacious and desirable opponents. In general, the names of salmon and trout – both seagoing species and those that live entirely in fresh water – are related to the Pacific Ocean when they are Pacific fish, and to corresponding salmonoids from the Atlantic when they are Atlantic fish.

Left: Big game fish are ever more often released, possibly after being tagged. Small billfish are commonly caught up by their jaws, instead of being gaffed, when they are to be tagged or set free.

Atlantic salmon

The species *Salmo salar* is a native of North Atlantic waters, ranging from the eastern Bay of Biscay up to the White Sea and the Baltic. It also occurs around Iceland and along southern Greenland. Previously it was found on the coasts of North America, from the Arctic Circle down to the Hudson River, but nowadays its southern limit is around New England. Moreover, it exists as a freshwater relic in a few areas of northern Europe and northeastern North America. Unfortunately the past 150 years of river exploitation, water pollution, and exhaustive fishing have wiped out very rich salmon stocks in their diverse environments on both sides of the Atlantic.

Trolling is possible for both salmon that are maturing and those that are migrating to spawn. It can be done by back trolling in rivers and trolling in archipelagos or in open waters.

I have matched the Grand Slam trio of Atlantic salmon in their respective surroundings at very different seasons. There have been fascinating encounters during quiet, bright Scandinavian summer nights in narrow river valleys, as well as frostbitten adventures on lakes with snow and rain in northerly winds during periods of fairly constant dusk. Unforgettable, too, has been fishing in a T-shirt on sunny surfaces that recalled the subtropics, even though I was zigzagging on open seas across the 56th parallel.

As a rule, when they emigrate in springtime, the young salmon (smolt) follow the surface currents of lakes and seas. Throughout their time at sea, they continue to hunt in the rich stretches of current, especially over deep water and at convergences of cold and warm water. Rises in the sea or lake floor, jut of land surrounded by currents, bays near deep water, and tributary flow into a bay are, therefore, good places for a salmon troller to cover.

During the spring, salmon run at the surface or close to it, both in the open sea and near land – and the smallest fish are usually highest up. Even during summer, the surface water can attract salmon as long as they find their optimum temperature there. But more commonly, and especially near land, they go and hunt in the thermocline. During the autumn, when the surface water becomes cool and mixed, salmon occur at all levels, occasionally just offshore. In late winter, the very coldest time of year, they head once again for deeper water.

The pre-spawning behavior of salmon is also fairly independent of their environment. They follow certain immigration routes to the spawning river. Usually the heavyweighters

arrive first – in some rivers already during early spring, in others during late autumn. Outside the river, in a fjord or a deep area, they tend to form groups of similar size and wait until the conditions are right for running upriver. Their appetite fades as they approach the river, but they do not entirely stop eating before they start upriver.

Atlantic Sea salmon

Salmon from the North Atlantic's tributaries follow the sea currents toward nutritious northerly waters just south of the Arctic Circle. There they get fat in the Norwegian Sea, around Iceland, and in the Davis Strait between Greenland and Canada. Their main prey are crustaceans, sand eels, stickleback and various species of herring. When returning to spawn, they weigh from 4 to 80 lbs (2-37 kg) depending on their age and genetic qualities.

In general, the troller makes contact with these salmon once they have headed toward their home coasts. They follow the ancient routes of immigration – which can vary with the season – along open coasts, fjord coasts, and skerries. Not seldom, their path is bordered by traps and gillnets, hinting at where a salmon troller should show his lures or baits. The fish may sneak toward the spawning river at some depth, or else approach it in the surface outflow from the river.

With the introduction of modern trolling techniques, rod catches along the Scandinavian west coast have grown steadily.

Pacific salmon

The genus *Oncorhynchus* consists of six species: the chinook (*O. tschawtyscha*), coho (*O. kisutch*), chum (*O. keta*), humpback (*O. gorbuscha*), sockeye (*O. nerka*) and cherry salmon (*O. masou*). However, the last species occurs only around Japan, and is regarded as a transitional form between salmon and trout.

All of these species originate in the Pacific area. but they have been introduced with varying success in different parts of the world. From the viewpoint of sportfishing, the best results with chinook and coho have been achieved in the Great Lakes.

Saltwater fishing

Off the west coast of North America, fishing waters are not stratified during the summer months in the same way as those of the Great Lakes. Instead, the locations of fish are influenced by upwelling water, powerful estuaries, and the tides. One can find maturing chinook hunting in small groups everywhere from the surface down to about 125 yds (m), especially where the temp-

erature is 12-14° C (53-57° F). Here they pursue large schools of anchovy, herring, alewife, smelt, squids and shrimp. They are most active around dawn, and then stay very high up in the water.

Moreover, they may move along bottoms at deep, rocky coasts, feeding on " rockfish" in the clefts. Usually the heaviest salmon of all can be found there. But both the forage fish and the predators could be difficult to detect with an echosounder on rocky bottoms.

The trailer line length is generally 30-65 ft (10-20 m) when the fish run shallow at 10-25 ft (3-8 m) or if the water is quite clear. However, a length of 13-23 ft (4-7m) may well be enough when the fish hunt deeper. It is therefore normal to stack the lures at intervals of 10-13 ft (3-4 m).

Chinook migrating to spawn are not so easily fooled, but they can be located without much trouble since they follow fixed routes – which, on the other hand, may shift with the seasons. Periodically a school pauses in deep holes or along slopes, where the fish prepare their bodies for the coming adaptation to a freshwater environment. As they stay very close to the bottom, your lure must be presented maximum a yard (meter) above it. The most successful West Coast trollers fish at extremely low speeds, sometimes so slowly that the boat barely holds against the tide. The lure – usually natural bait – then rotates lazily and attractively in the current.

Such slow speed provides a fine opportunity to use dodgers in front of the lure or bait. It is thought that the salmon mistake the attractor's sound and shimmer for a competing fish. Often the very biggest salmon are the ones that strike near the bottom during slow trolling. The leader between the attractor and lure or bait is abnormally long – at least a rod length in most cases.

Freshwater fishing

As a rule, the fishing season in Lakes Michigan and Ontario lasts from the end of April to mid-October. The chinook feed mainly on alewife and smelt – but predominantly the latter in Lake Ontario, as shown by analysis of stomach contents.

During the spring, the fish hunt in small schools near the surface over deep waters. When the lakes stratify in summertime, the chinooks head for the thermocline, which is usually about 65 ft (20 m) deep. They occur both in the thermocline and around its upper limit, preferring a temperature of 13° C (55° F). Very seldom do we find freshwater chinooks at the bottom. They also tend to stay half a nautical mile or so from the shores, unless winds push cold water along the shores.

Stocking of Pacific salmon in the Great Lakes has given birth to a huge sportfishing industry. Local tourism generates several billion dollars annually, and has led to charter-boat operations with well-equipped vessels of the size shown here in every harbor. This makes it possible for one and all to try a hand at salmon trolling.

In late summer and autumn, the fish become ever more densely concentrated outside the river mouths. They prepare to run upriver and spawn, which means that they often lose their appetites. Nevertheless, very large chinooks are taken every year at this time.

The troller should know when and where the fish occur under different conditions. He finds these spots with the help of a navigator, always looking for breakpoints over them. These may be where two currents meet, where the temperature shifts for some reason, or where the bottom slopes sharply. To the troller, even dawn and dusk are breakpoints in the life of the fish.

Since the chinook pursue schools of smelt and alewife, they occur around the river mouths in springtime when the latter are spawning, not least in the edge slicks between the outflow river water and the lake water. During the summer, the forage fish are pelagic, according to the temperature and the supply of plankton. These factors can make the fishing quite unpredictable, but it is always challenging. In autumn, river-mouth fishing is emphasized on both Lakes Michigan and Ontario.

To put things briefly, the surface-going spring salmon in Lake Ontario are tempted with fish-imitating plugs, while the salmon that move in the thermocline tend to fall for light Sutton spoons and attractor/squids combinations. The last of these, together with flatnosed plugs, usually work well during the late season, when strong colors with some blue and green are effective. Line lengths and trolling speeds are, once again, adjusted to the fishing depth and visibility, the water conditions and type of lure, as well as the time of year.

In regard to plugs, my impression from chinook fishing on the Great Lakes is that plugs, such as the silver J-plug with blue and green features, are the most common and successful. Small J-plugs or alike (Nos. 2 and 3) are sometimes also used behind dodgers (No. 0 or 1); the separation should be 20-40 inches (50-100 cm) for the lure to acquire the right erratic run. Large J-plugs are run directly from a flatline or on a downrigger, but they can also be profitably pulled on a leader of 48-72 in (120-180 cm) behind a diving planer.

Trout and steelhead

Brown trout (*Salmo trutta*) are native to Europe, and rainbow trout (*Oncorhynchus mykiss*) to North America. They both exist in purely freshwater variants as well as in seagoing ones. Brown trout occur in many forms, adapted to their particular environments. In European waters they inhabit not only brooks and lakes but also the Baltic and the North Sea. Their inland varieties grow especially large, and specimens of around 44 lbs (20 kg) have been caught.

Lake-run and sea-going trout acquire a silvery gleam as they grow, and they darken when preparing to spawn. But the latter appearance varies, and it can be hard to distinguish large-sized silvery trout from the Atlantic salmon.. One can identify these species most certainly by studying the gill-raker teeth, which are all rod-shaped on the first gill arch in salmon, but are partly knob-shaped in trout.

Sea-going trout

The majority of sea-going trout are not open water fish to the same extent as salmon. Regardless of the season, they stay very close to cliffs and stones, shifting position with the wind and current directions. They enjoy windward shores, and may come right up to land with an onshore wind. But in a constant offshore wind, they move farther out towards more structure bottoms.

All sea trout run up their spawning rivers during the summer and autumn. Most survive their spawning period and return to the ocean. According to taggings, though, they seldom migrate far during their second period at sea, but tend to linger near their spawning rivers.

Trolling fishermen after trophy trout should concentrate on the waters outside well-known rivers of this kind – where herring, sand eels, stickleback, smelt and crustaceans occur. The bottoms may consist of shallow stony ridges, or of sand and gravel interspersed with weed-grown boulders. Here the trout often reside from autumn until spring, especially if there is a warm-water outflow in the vicinity.

Suspended trout usually gorge on schools of herring where the depth is 30-80 ft (10-25 m). As a rule they hunt the herring high up, in the top half of the water. They may also occur in summertime around skerries at such depths, as well as jut of land and islands in strong currents, when the water near land becomes warm.

It is easiest to make contact with sea trout when the temperature is 5-10° C (41-50° F). During the dark months, the fishing is usually best in the middle of the day; but later in the season, the trout are most active at dawn and dusk. Then, and during the night, they go very shallow. In Sweden, the majority of large coastal trout, weighing 22-30 lbs (10-14 kg), are caught over shallow, stony, current-swept bottoms in springtime.

Lake-run trout

Cold, clear lakes are inhabited by large-sized trout that behave much like sea-going trout. They swim near the surface in spring and autumn, often in shallow waters near shore. During the summer months, though, they prefer deep slopes where upwelling cold, nutritious bottom water provides the ideal temperature and attracts prey fish. There, they may hunt very deep in the daytime, but also make occasional shoreward raids at night.

On the other hand, lake-run trout are not as happy as sea-going trout to stay over shallow bottoms during the winter, since the shore waters of lakes are then much colder than sea water. It is only when warm spots arise for various reasons, close to land during the late winter and spring, that lake trout concentrate here. As young the trout live on diverse small animals – but as they grow, their diet turns to fish foods such as smelt, vendace, perch fry and stickleback.

In Ireland and Scotland, lake trolling with flies is popular during the spring. The "loch trout" rarely grows to great size, but its colorfulness is impressive.

A variety of techniques

Trolling for trout is many-folded and usually very instructive. Depending on the environment and time of year, it can be done by simply rowing with a flatline, or by advanced forms of deep trolling.

Planer-board fishing is an efficient technique when it comes to shallow-hunting and shy trout. One can seldom get more lessons or enjoyment from this technique than in springtime, when the trout are hiding close to isolated boulders, or else going so shallow that a boat keel cannot follow them. It is then a real test of precision for both the boat and your equipment.

A downrigger, too, serves well when the lure is to be presented near the surface in salt water – even there is a lot of grass and weeds in the water, since the wire and line collect most of the rubbish in front of the lure. Fishing with a downrigger near the surface, though, usually requires a long line of 100-165 ft (30-50 m), especially if the water is clear, shallow and calm.

Elsewhere, the downrigger and diving planer are unbeatable for showing a lure to suspended trout that hunt herring, or bringing the lure in close to steep shores or cliff shelves. But if the trout are feeding at depths of 30-50 ft (10-15 m), a line length of around 15 ft (5 m) should be enough. Then, too, the thinnest flutterspoons are normally very attractive on short lines behind a downrigger. The best distance between diving planer and lure is about 6 ft (180 cm).

Trout have a diverse diet, so you need a wide range of lures. They tend to prefer lures measuring 2-6 inches (5-15 cm).

Sometimes, however, they are highly selective and just gape at a particular type, size and color of lure. My own trout box is dominated by plugs and spoons, while I prefer silvery lures in the sea and warmer colors in fresh water. A tube fly, squid, or imitation sand eel, behind an attractor presented at depth, may also entice a strike.

The trolling speed must be adjusted to your lure or bait.. Trout are not as fast and mobile at midwinter as, for example, in June; so the speedometer ought to read at most 2 knots in winter. But a lure pulled at 3 knots is no problem for spring trout to inspect long and hard.

A trout troller's equipment should be in the light to medium class. It is really only when fishing with a diving planer that one needs somewhat heavier gear. To spread the lines better and reach shy fish as well, there may be reason to use rods 10-12 feet long at the sides, whereas downrigger rods are usually 8-9 feet long.

Trout can tear the lure from the line release with the same violence as do salmon. Yet they do not rush as far or, therefore, bend the rod into the same steady curve. Instead, they show their strength with brief opposition and short, quick rushes, which make the rod bow often and deeply. Nor are they averse to exposing themselves in leaps, when the water warms up during summer and autumn. In springtime they are more inclined to roll at the surface. My personal judgment is that "small" trout of 10-12 lbs (4-5 kg) are about as pugnacious as a salmon of similar size.

Steelhead

Steelhead is the seagoing variety of *Oncorhynchus mykiss*, the freshwater rainbow trout. Both of these originate in western North America. Rainbow trout are said to be the world's most widespread sportfish.

The steelhead was named for its gray head. In the sea and in large deep lakes, it has a gray-blue back, and is as shiny along the sides as salmon and brown trout. However, it is slimmer in shape than the often chubby rainbow trout. That it, too, can grow very big is shown by the fact that a giant of 42.lb 2 oz (19.1 kg) has been caught by rod in Alaska.

The Skamania steelhead is certainly among the most spectacular salmonoids that can be hooked. Steelhead reputedly prefer water with a temperature of 14.5-16.5° C (58-62° F). Investigations in the Great Lakes have shown that, during the winter, they linger rather passively in deep water around 4° C

(39° F), although when the surface water near land reaches 5.5-6.5° C (42-44° F) they head for it to hunt small prey.

As the temperature rises, they move out into the lake, and are glad to stay where it reaches 7-9° C (45-48° F). They increase in appetite and activity while approaching their summer residence, in the surface layer over deep waters up to 20 nautical miles from land.

Trollers look for steelhead in and around spots of calm water, slicks at open water whirlpools where rubbish collects, and in misty areas. These are usually visible signs of temperature changes in the water.

Fish that regularly cruise in the surface layer tend to be very watchful and shy. The normal recipe for activating the fish is a long line, either hanging from the rod tip or attached to a planer board or downrigger. During the spring, effective lures are slim silvery plugs, 4-6 inches (10-15 cm) long, such as the Cisco Kid, Bomber and Rapala. But in summertime, steelhead – unlike other salmonoids – are often willing to take at midday and swallow a wide range of lures; they seem most partial to red-orange, fish-imittating plugs. Autumn fishing along coasts and river mouths, in dark shore water, is made attractive with fluorescent colors. Slow trolling with Flatfish, Kwikfish and Tadpolly on the line has also paid off.

Many American trollers speak warmly of light-line fishing for steelhead. They fish with soft 12-foot "noodle rods", which are densely ringed and, in some cases, have pliable guides that prevent the line from rubbing against the rod. On the trolling reel is monoline of 2-6 lbs (0.13-0.23 mm) and there may be a small swivel at the line end. Usually a featherlight lure with an extremely sharpened hook is knotted directly to the reel line, with no shock leader in front. Rubberbands are the only line releases used. Every year on this light equipment, the enthusiasts take not only large-sized steelhead.

Rainbow trout, steelhead and other salmonoids are caught during the winter half-year by harling on the faster-flowing stretches of spawning rivers. This is generally done in dory-like "drift boats", light 16-foot aluminum craft that are excellent fishing platforms on water with swift currents and many rapids. The oarsman cover the river from bank to bank, while letting the boat go slowly downstream. An identical technique is used in Scandinavia. The fishing passenger(s) can drag natural bait – such as salmon roe – or spoons, spinners and wobblers, 30-65 feet (10-20 m) behind the boat

Char

The genus *Salvelinus*, which prefers cold water, is wide-spread in the Northern Hemisphere, chiefly in North America. Among its fifteen-odd species, the most popular sportfish are char (*S. alpinus*), lake trout (*S. namaycush*) and brool trout (*S. fontinalis*). Few sportfish can compare with them in beauty. The first two species are of prime interest to trollers.

Char exist on both sides of the Atlantic, in both freshwater and seagoing varieties. The freshwater kind can grow almost as big as the latter, reaching weights of well over 20 lbs (10 kg). Char require clear, cold water with a high pH value, and their optimum temperature is 5-13° C (41-55° F). Big chars usual diet consists of smelt, vendace, stickleback and perch fry.

Sea-going Arctic char live, for example, along the North Atlantic coast of the Scandinavian peninsula and in the Northwest Territory of Canada. Primarily nourished by fish and crustaceans, they have been rod-caught in weights up to 32.5 lbs (14.77 kg).

Large char can be found at all levels in the water during its spring and autumn circulation in northerly lakes. As the water warms up in summertime, the fish move out to deep areas, mostly in the lower limit of the thermocline or beneath it. Consequently, a troller often encounters it over banks swept by bottom currents, or along deep edges at 100-130 ft (30-40 m).

The active hours of char are less restricted to dawn and dusk than in the case of other salmonoids. This is because the light, which can barely penetrate down to the depths where char live, does not determine the urge to hunt as much as it does in higher water layers. The fishing may prove ideal on a sunny afternoon with a rippled surface. It is especially good during longer periods of high pressure, notably before the autumn spawning time.

Lures can be placed at the char's level with a wire line or a diving planer. But the best aid is a downrigger, not least if you have to go deeper than 165 ft (50 m). Attractors seem to draw the char more strongly than other fish. A string of "mini-cowbells", with a worm on the hook, is the traditional and so far the commonest method. In larger lakes, it is thought most effective to use a mother-of-pearl spinner on the end of a "magnum cowbell". You should troll slowly at 1.5-2 knots.

Lake trout, the giants of the genus, have been introduced in deep lakes in Europé. However, despite their substantial weight, they are not yet near the specimen of 102 lbs (46.3 kg) which has been caught in Canada. Rod caught examples up to 65 lbs (29.48 kg) are known from Great Bear Lake.

Usually lake trout are dark brown-green to light gray, with light patches. They live in deep cold lakes, preferably at temperatures of 7-13° C (44-55° F). So they may appear in shallow water during the spring and autumn – but as a rule they hunt in small groups at deep edges and in holes. Already when 6-8 inches (15-20 cm) long, they turn to fish food, mainly vendace and smelt.

Downriggers are the perfect approach to lake trout. While a number of fishermen still pull down the lure with wire line, most of us definitely call for a downrigger and rods of 8-9 feet with medium to stiff action. At the end of the 0.35-0.40 mm line (20 lb), and 1-5 ft (30-150 cm) in front of the lure – a plug, spoon, or plastic imitation – is usually a chromed attractor or cowbell that stimulates the fish with sight and sound. Remember that, by keeping a slow , bouncing the bottom with your weight and jigging with the rod tip, you can soon transform the fish's curiosity about the lure into a strike.

Lake trout are heavy fighters. What they tend to offer are not long rushes or abrupt leaps, but strong resistance when you are pumping a 20-lb (10-kg) specimen out of the depths. And the very feeling of its power along the downrigger rod's handle, when it stops and shakes its head to get rid of the lure, can be just as nerve-wracking as a fish that runs around the boat on the surface. You fight "blind" without knowing how the lure is sitting, unable to follow its course so easily. Thus, lake trout are in many ways an extra, peculiar "spice" on the table of trolling in European waters.

Pikeperch/Walleye

Pikeperch belong to the perch family (*Percidae*) and are restricted to the Northern Hemisphere (Europe, Asia and North America). Most species of pikeperch live in fresh water, some in brackish water, and only one in salt water. The "European" pikeperch, the zander (Stizostedion lucioperka) is the biggest in this group. It has been rod-caught in weights up to 40.5 lbs (18.37 kg) in Germany. Among the North American species are the walleye (*S. vitreum vitreum*), which is registered up to 24 lbs (11 kg), and the much smaller sauger (*S. canadense*).

Pikeperch have appealed increasingly to sportfishermen during recent decades. They are now caught year-round by various methods in both fresh and brakish waters. Most of the big ones are taken by trolling in the high-pressure periods of summer, when the nocturnal fish hunt very close to the surface. As long as the sun is above the horizon, the pikeperch usually stay deep

The steelhead is the seagoing variety of rainbow trout. Native to western North America, it has been successfully stocked in the Great Lakes. Today it also occurs increasingly in the Baltic Sea. Specimens of over 42 lbs (19 kg) have been rod-caught in Alaska. On the hook, a steelhead is a glistening package of power. Often you see this lightning-fast fish jumping high in the air before the reel-clicker lets you know that something has taken your lure.

in clear lakes. But in murky flatland lakes, with its excellent sight, it may begin to hunt near the surface long before dusk. Small pikeperch hunt in modest groups, and larger ones either alone or in pairs. Spring and autumn, too, may find them in the upper water layers during the early dawn hours and evenings.

Pikeperch hunt not only in the free waters, but also in the shallows along coasts. They like oxygen-rich water with short vegetation, over both soft and hard bottoms. In deep areas they normally stay near the bottom, but during the summer they seldom linger under the thermocline.

At night, pikeperch tend to take for longer and more intensive periods than in the daytime. They seem to rest for an hour or so

after sundown, then launch a frantic hunt for bleak, roach, smelt, and small fish of their own kind. They prefer a water temperature of 11-23° C (52-73° F), ideally just under 20° C (68° F).

Slow surface trolling with light, noisy plugs is the traditional and still predominant method of fishing for pikeperch during the summer in Scandinavian countries. But spoons and natural bait (smelt, vendace) also have many advocates there. In North America, it is more common to use "walleye spinners" tipped with nightcrawlers. Pikeperch take carefully, sneaking up to the lure and gladly swimming along with it. You should watch the rod tips closely, use very sharp hooks, and fish with line that is as short and stiff as possible.

Arctic char are among the loveliest fish that can be hooked. Whether you are after land-locked Arctic char or North American lake trout (at right), you should present the lure deep.

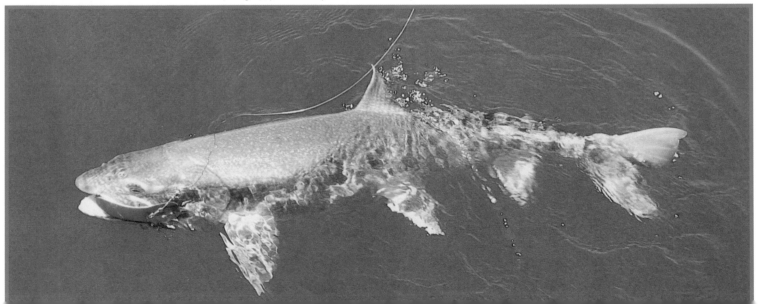

In the United States, year-round fishing for walleye is far more widespread than its counterpart in Scandinavia, no doubt since the sport is more developed. When downrigger fishing for walleye was introduced to Lake Erie, the catches temporarily increased by 15%.

Downrigger fishing is unlike the surface trolling in regard to speed, among other things. The best catches have been made with light flutterspoons, pulled at 2.5-3.5 knots. There should be at least 50 ft (15 m) between the line release and the lure.

The downrigger's effectiveness

Walleye are an almost unbelievably prized sportfish in some parts of North America, especially around Lake Erie in the USA and Ontario in Canada. During the late 1970s, when people began to fish for walleye with downriggers in Lake Erie, the catches grew by an average 15% during late summer and autumn. However, the walleye behaves somewhat differently from Europe's zander. Except in the Great Lakes, it seems to be more bottom-living, although this does not mean it is a deep-water fish.

The spring fishing takes place in shallow waters, but downriggers are used even then. When the depth reaches 5-23 ft (1.5-7 m), the lures (plugs, spoons and natural bait) are released 50-100 ft (15-30 m) behind the boat. In shallow water – where the walleyes are easy to frighten – it is still more common to present the lure with in-line planer boards, or else

directly from a flatline. Only when fish move to deeper water during the summer, at a fishing depth of 30-65 ft (10-20 m), does the downrigger become really effective. Usually the line is 30-50 ft (10-15 m) long at first, but can be shortened while you are fishing. In large lakes, the lures are often stacked to find the right depths for walleye.

Special line releases are generally used for pikeperch fishing, which are a little more sensitive than those for traditional salmon fishing. The trolling speed is dictated by the water temperature: under 10° C (50° F), a typical speed is 1.6-2.1 knots, whereas above 15° C (59° F) the speed should be 2.5-3 knots.

A guide to choosing the lure is that you should fish with dark lures on cloudy days, and bright lures on clear days. Be sure to present the lures at, or just above, the level where the fish hunt – which, as mentioned, is usually the bottom in the USA. Remember, too, that pikeperch / walleye have a strong tendency to hunt from below.

Pike

The pike family (*Esocidae*) comprises five species. Only one of them, the widespread northern pike (*Esox lucius*), also lives in Europe. Another, weighing at most 22 lbs (10 kg), occurs in Eurasia (*E. reicherti*). Those found in eastern North America are the chain pickerel (*E. niger*), the redfin or grass pickerel (*E. americanus*), and the muskellunge (*E. masquinongy*).

Heaviest is the musky, at about 110 lbs (50 kg), but northern pike weigh up to 77 lbs (35 kg). It is said that no more beautiful – or tough – Esox-fish can be hooked than the "tiger musky", a cross between a male northern pike and a female musky. Such hybrids sometimes occur spontaneously in the wild, and they can reach weights of 50 lbs (22.7 kg).

The world's finest stocks of pike are probably those available to trollers in Sweden. This is suggested at least by their catch statistics. The pike in Sweden are spread over almost the whole country.

The eating habits of pike depend on their size. The smaller they are, the more often they take. An old pike can digest food for a week, before stuffing itself again in a few hectic hours.

Pike generally stay close to shores or bottoms, except in large deep lakes and in the Baltic Sea. Here, a salmon or trout troller occasionally comes to grips with big suspended pike that hunt in open waters. Their stomach contents show that they have feasted on schools of vendace or herring. Normally the pike stay beyond the vegetation belt. Among their favorite haunts in springtime are the shallow areas outside estuaries.

In autumn, when coastal waters get cold again, the pike linger at depths of 6-26 ft (2-8 m). But during the coldest season, they reappear far down, where the water is warmest.

Most pike trollers comb the bottoms and deep edges with large, often colorful plugs, 6-12 inches (15-30 cm) long, pulled 65-100 ft (20-30 m) behind the boat.

The trolling set-up may include a couple of rods 6-7 feet long that point straight astern, and a couple 9-11 feet long that stick out from the sides. Be sure that the rods are parallel to the water surface, since this offers minimum wind resistance on your line, as well as maximum chances of hooking the pike when they take. The reel drag is adjusted to the lure's size. Usually the fish are hooked by the boat's speed, so it is important to give them enough line. Still, you should respond with an extra strike.

A pike troller must try to fish with the stiffest (non-stretchy) possible line, separating it from the bait with a leader 12-20 inches (30-50 cm) long, of nylon-covered wire or thick monofilament.

On an increasing number of pike-trolling boats, there is also a downrigger that can place the lure more exactly at the right depth, and can make the hooking more effective. It also enables you to fish with lighter equipment.

Musky

The gigantic musky is a lot more bewitching to North American fishermen than is the northern pike in Europe. Muskies are spring-spawning and once existed only in the northeastern USA, mainly around the Great Lakes, but they have been introduced in many other waters. According to many musky fishermen, the really big ones, exceeding 40 lbs (18 kg), must be taken by trolling.

A musky stays protected, and attacks the lure from its "hideout"; so you have to present the lure at a holding station, which is its more or less permanent feeding site. Big muskies usually occur at a rocky deep edge, a grassy sandbank at the junction of two tributaries, or a current-swept jut of land that may well be rich in vegetation. Rarely going deeper than 40 ft (12 m), they have an optimum temperature of 10-20° C (50-68° F).

Top: *Pike cannot be confused with any other Scandinavian fish. But their body colors and patterns may depend greatly on where they are caught.*
Bottom: *The musky is the giant of the pike family. Weighing up to around 110 lbs (50 kg), it originated in eastern North America, where few other fish can match it in legendary fame - or in terms of advice about how to troll for it. One agreed fact is that the trolling lures should be large, tough and sharp, like the fish itself.*

This bluefin tuna weighing 700 lbs (320 kg) was boarded after a four-hour fight, off Puerto Rico on Grand Canary. At the first irresistible rush toward the continental cliff, it tore 600 metres of line from the reel, which shot up in temperature and sang the highest note of its career.

A musky is not shy when it comes to eating the forage fish that pass by such places. These include pikeperch/walleye, perch and bass – ideally of good size, so that the musky soon eats its fill.

Autumn is the best time for fishing muskies. It is common to troll with 3-4 rods, 6-7 feet long with a lot of backbone and fast tip. The majority of fishermen use multiplier reels holding around

150 yards of monoline 12-20 lb (0.30-0.40 mm). Classic lures are the Swim Whizz and the "Muskie Bug"; other large, floating, deep-going plugs are also appreciated. The trolling speed depends on the season, but is normally 2.5-3.5 knots. There is no need for very long lines, 10-25 yards being an accepted distance.

Tuna

The 13 species of tuna belong to the large mackerel family. Usually living in flocks or schools, they occur in warm temperate seas around the world. Popular heavies in the family are the bluefin, the yellowfin and the bigeye tuna. They occur together in many places, and I myself have met all three of those species in unforgettable fights in widely separated waters.

Tuna are warm-blooded and have a "heat-exchanger" which can keep their bodies at least 10° C (18° F) warmer than the surrounding water. This enormous tolerance is reflected by the bluefins tunas ability to feed in water with a temperature of only 4.5° C (40° F) in northern latitudes, even though they spawn in tropical waters at 30° C (86° F).

Bluefin tuna

The bluefin tuna (*Thunnus thynnus*) is the largest of all tunafish. Giants of nearly 1,540 lbs (700 kg), 13 yds (4 m) long, have been caught by commercial fishermen, and the rod record is no less than 1,497 lbs (679 kg).

Unfortunately, the bluefin tuna's existence is facing serious threats. The reason is commercial slaughter fishing. The bluefin occurs in subtropical and temperate waters of the North Pacific Ocean, the North Atlantic Ocean and in the Mediterrannean and Black Sea.

There are several varieties of bluefin tuna, named after the Southern, Northern, Western, and Eastern Atlantic regions. They undertake transoceanic migrations, The Northern Atlantic bluefin is certainly the largest.

To match a "jumbo maguro" one do best heading for the east coast of North America. For Europeans, the best choices are the Canaries, Madeira or the Azores – and the Mediterranean offers bluefin tuna of diverse sizes.

When fishing for bluefin tuna, you should use heavy class equipment. The rods will have lever-drag reels and monofilament line in the same IGFA classes. The reel drag should be adjusted to one-third of the line's breaking strength. Also on board should be accessories such as a well-oiled fighting chair, harnesses, flying gaff and tail rope.

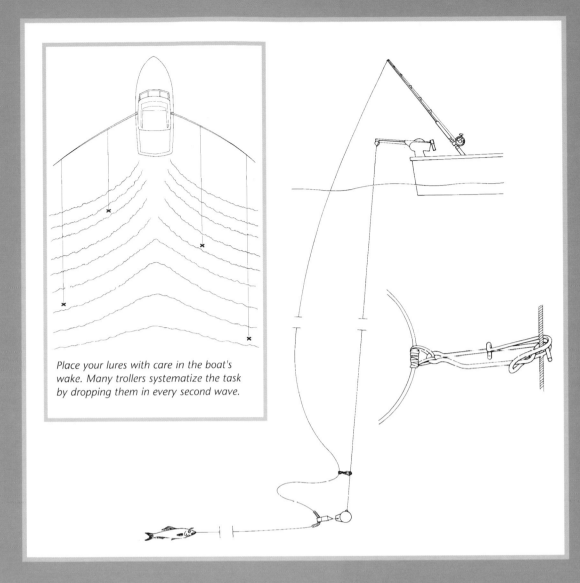

Place your lures with care in the boat's wake. Many trollers systematize the task by dropping them in every second wave.

A fish finds most of its food in the depths. But presenting a live bait down there is much harder than at the surface. Downriggers have thus created new opportunities. To give the fish slack line and time for swallowing, the bait is provided with two line releases. A bridle-rigged mackerel, or a small tuna, swims about 165 ft (50 m) behind the lower release, which sits on the weight. It can be a good idea to wrap the fishing line with wax thread where the line release clamps on, both to protect the line and to keep track of the dragging distance. The dropback loop between the two releases can vary in length, but is normally half as long as the drag distance to the bait. The upper release is a halibut snap, with one end coupled to the downrigger wire, and the other attached to the fishing line by a No.64 rubberband. You should carefully lower the tackle to the desired depth, then tighten the line between the upper release and the reel.

The lure or bait can be presented either with a downrigger or by direct flatline fishing. As long as you use natural bait, the boat should move rather slowly at 3-6 knots. From outriggers, you can also fish with spreader bars or daisy chains, at least 130-165 ft (40-50 m) behind the boat. The third spreader rig should point astern and have a line length of 65-80 ft (20-25 m). Baits – herring, coalfish, mackerel or squid – should run at the surface. With this triple set-up, which might consist of two mackerel rigs and a squid rig, the tuna should get the impression that a school is following the boat. Attractors can be plastic squids or natural bait, the latter being attached to the leader with closed mouths.

When a tuna takes a surface-going lure, the hook can be driven in hard with an extra jab at the throttle, and your rod tip will show the result. Then you have to bring the other lures home, before concentrating on how to maneuver the boat and play the fish. This is often a revealing moment as regards the condition of the fish, fisherman and equipment alike.

Big game on downriggers

Downrigger fishing for tuna becomes increasingly popular nowadays, and logically so, as the fish tend to feed deep. In recent years a number of impressive bluefin tuna have been caught off the northeastern USA, mostly at 50-100 ft (15-30 m).

Once a tuna is on the hook, you need to clean up fast on board. Thus many big-game fishermen prefer rapid electric downriggers, mounted on swivel bases and quick mount adapter for instant mounting in flush rod-holders at the side deck. The downriggers are then easy to stick in and lift out.

Rubberbands are good, cheap line releases in salt water. The following arrangement is suitable for many other big game fish in addition to tuna.

If the fish needs slack line when it takes – which tuna seldom do – you should place two line releases on the line, one above the other. Then feed out the lure to the desired trailer length, which depends for instance on the lure's size and on whether it is alive or dead. Fasten the line in the weight's line release, perhaps rein-

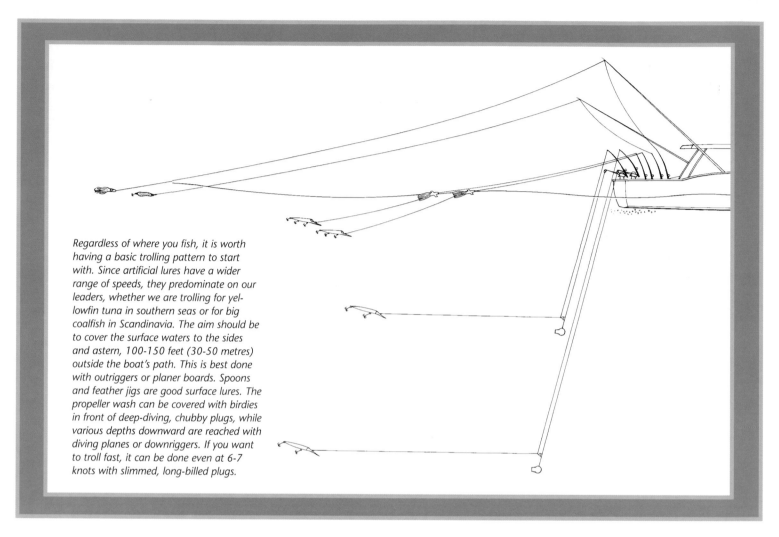

Regardless of where you fish, it is worth having a basic trolling pattern to start with. Since artificial lures have a wider range of speeds, they predominate on our leaders, whether we are trolling for yellowfin tuna in southern seas or for big coalfish in Scandinavia. The aim should be to cover the surface waters to the sides and astern, 100-150 feet (30-50 metres) outside the boat's path. This is best done with outriggers or planer boards. Spoons and feather jigs are good surface lures. The propeller wash can be covered with birdies in front of deep-diving, chubby plugs, while various depths downward are reached with diving planes or downriggers. If you want to troll fast, it can be done even at 6-7 knots with slimmed, long-billed plugs.

forced by an extra rubberband. Sink it 20-40 inches (50-100 cm) under the surface, and feed out the slack line that seems necessary in view of the lure's distance behind the boat. Next, reattach the reel line to the wire with a rubberband – which should be wound several times on the line to prevent slipping. Some skippers use a halibut clamp between the rubberband and the wire.

Lower the lure carefully to the chosen depth. This is especially important when you use live bait. Tighten up the reel line between the rod tip and the upper release, to minimize slack line here. The reel's line-out alarm should be turned on, and the drag set lightly – not a bit harder than in the strike position.

As the fish takes the lure and jerks line from the lower release, it feels almost no resistance because of the slack line, and is thus unlikely to spit out the lure. Only when the slack line has stretched out does the fish encounter resistance, due to the other release and the boat's motion. These forces will hopefully hook the fish before the rubberband breaks and the reel click signals that the first round has begun.

Tuna have flexible diets, but proven baits in both deep and surface waters are the mackerel, bluefish and gray mullet. Live baits will keep longest and move best if they are bridle-rigged. Artificial lures used in salt water for downrigger fishing are usually big plugs, spoons, plastic lures and feather jigs. But make sure that the hooks and their attachments can stand the expected wear.

With artificial lures on the line end, no "drop-back" effect is attempted, but you should clamp the line hard in the single release used. Further, tighten up the reel line as much as possible against the release, and put the reel drag in the strike position.

Yellowfin tuna

A downrigger can also be used to present tuna lures in or near the surface. Artificial lures are usually very effective when fishing for tuna that live in schools, including small bluefin tuna. Where they swim in large schools, their hunting is revealed by the presence of diving gulls and white spray on the surface.

In such situations the yellowfin tuna (*Thunnus albacares*) is among the most impressive fish, whether it is hunting or fighting hooked. Many of us consider the yellowfin, pound for pound, to be the toughest quarry a sportfisherman can match, especially if it is in the 200-lb (100-kg) class. Add to this its amazing beauty, and the fact that it is sometimes nearly impossible to tempt – generally because of its strong concentration on a particular type of food, which may be far smaller than the fish itself, such as baby squids. Thus, even on the open sea, you must "match the hatch" to make the rod tip bend. White feather lures, small or medium-size kona heads, knuckleheads and psychobeads, as well as mackerel, gray mullet and garfish, are undoubtedly reliable here.

Yellowfin tuna occur in the warm temperate oceans, and can reach weights of almost 440 lbs (200 kg. As the name shows, this fish has golden yellow fins.

Fighting the yellowfin tuna is most enjoyable on IGFA class 30-50 equipment, particularly if it can be coaxed to take a surface-going artificial lure. It then tends to begin with a long rush near the surface, followed by a sudden dive against the depth – which may seem bottomless as the fish tears line from the reel.

Bigeye tuna

The bigeye tuna (*Thunnus obesus)* is found in tropical and sub-tropical seas, except the Mediterranean. It partly recalls the yellowfin tuna, of which it was long regarded as a variant.

Bigeye tuna are pelagic wanderers, and – unlike the bluefin and yellowfin tuna – they prefer deep waters during the day. Their backs are dark blue and their sides silvery. Off Cabo Blanco, Peru, they have been rod-caught in weights up to 435 lbs (197.31 kg). This is probably close to their maximum weight.

Bigeye tuna feed on small mackerel, gray mullet, sardines, squids, shellfish; and certain deep-water species. They are caught from boats by trolling deep with small natural bait – such as squids, gray mullet and mackerel. Artificial lures appeal to them in about the same variety as with yellowfin tuna. However, it is usually only the smaller fish that take such lures near the surface.

An incredibly tough fighter, the bigeye tuna battles intensely and is glad to do so on a long line in the dark layers of the sea. It can quickly regain strength, even after long rushes in cold deep water.

Sharks

Sharks rule a wide realm in the world's seas, and some of their species are prominent trolling fish – mainly the mako and porbeagle, though others can also be caught on trolling lures. The mako shark has a global distribution in tropical and warm temperate oceans. No trolling fish is so greatly respected as the mako. This enormously versatile and aggressive fish can jump around 30 ft (10 m) above the surface when hooked and reach weights of about 1,550 lbs (700 kg).

The mako shark is one of the wildest fish that can take a trolling lure. Many sport- fishermen harbor a kind of hatred for this unpredictable, aggressive racer, which can also leap higher than any other sportfish.

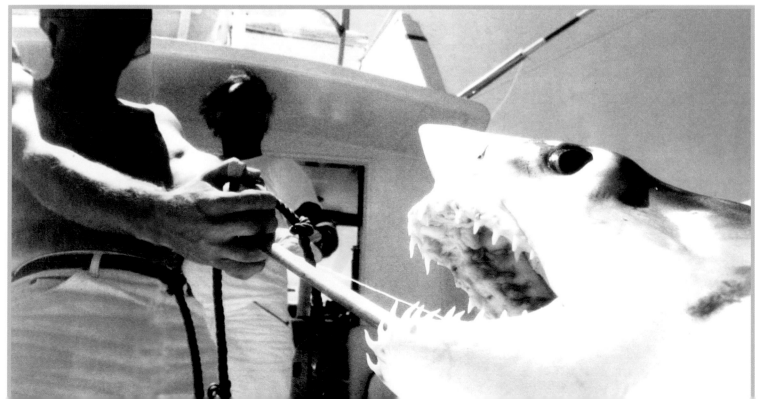

The mako is a fast-swimming, warm-blooded solitary hunter, and eats most kinds of popular trolling fish that cross its path. Makos are caught by either surface or deep trolling; they take artificial as well as natural baits, pulled at 2-5 knots. Capricious in ways of attacking, they sometimes strike without hesitation, but occasionally call for a drop-back effect to be hooked. When they are caught on a down-rigger, the tension in the line release should be set hard, and the distance from it to the lure should be short – about 16 ft (5 m). Usually a couple of extra strikes are needed to drive the hook in strongly.

The porbeagle shark is a close relative of the mako, but can be distinguished by its teeth, fin positions, and darker blue-gray color. Nor does it grow as large: the max weight is about 500 lb (225 kg) This species (*Lamna nasus*) is found in cold to temperate waters of the Pacific and North Atlantic Oceans, and in the Mediterranean. The porbeagle is feeding on herring, mackerel, coalfish and squids at different levels.

Off the rocky coast of Ireland mackerel baits are trolled at about 10 ft (3 m) down and 200 ft (60 m) behind the boat, whose speed is 2-4 knots. A trolled porbeagle fights better than a driftfished one, because the hook sits farther forward in its jaw.

A successful shark tackle, at the end of IGFA class 30-50 lbs (15-24 kg) equipment, may consist of a double-hook arrangement in sizes 8/0 and 9/0, for a mackerel measuring 10-12 inches (25-30 cm). One hook is inserted through the underjaw, then through the upper jaw, while the other is tied to the tail spool with rubber-bands. Between the hook and reel line is a stainless-steel wire, 10-15 feet long, of test strength 300 lbs, and the fishing line is attached to the wire by a roller-bearing snap swivel (200-300 lbs).

Billfish

Billfish – the sailfish, spearfish, swordfish and marlin – occur at southerly latitudes, as in Australia, New Zealand, Africa, the Canaries and Azores, Venezuela, Peru, Costa Rica, Mexico, the USA and Hawaii, Cuba and other islands in the Caribbean. Such "hot spots" are attracting ever more of us to meet these gladiators of the fish world.

Billfish, the gladiators of the fishing world, are a jump-happy and pugnacious family. Their spectacular performances can make the fisherman's shriek as shrill as his reel's.

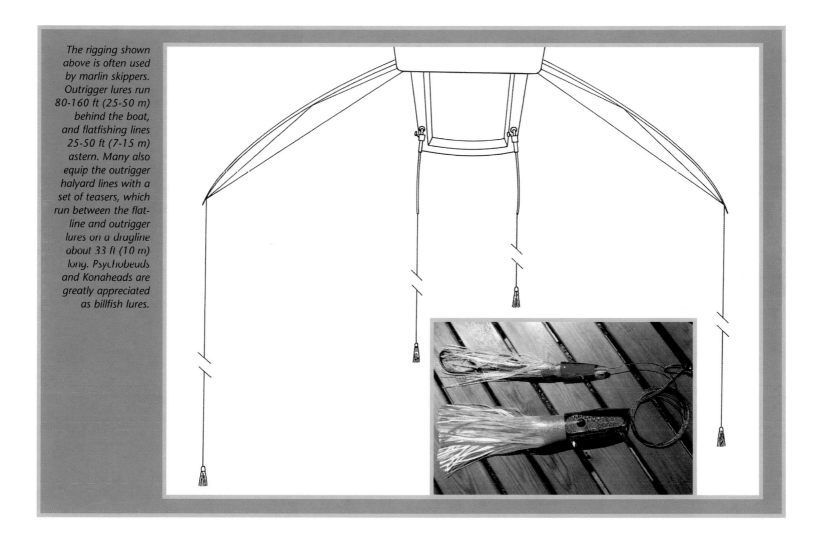

The rigging shown above is often used by marlin skippers. Outrigger lures run 80-160 ft (25-50 m) behind the boat, and flatfishing lines 25-50 ft (7-15 m) astern. Many also equip the outrigger halyard lines with a set of teasers, which run between the flat-line and outrigger lures on a dragline about 33 ft (10 m) long. Psychobeads and Konaheads are greatly appreciated as billfish lures.

Sailfish

The sailfish (*Istiophorus platypterus*) lives in tropical and sub-tropical seas, at temperatures of 22-30° C (71-90° F). Its name is due to the front dorsal fin, which it raises to a height twice that of its own body. Sailfish grow rapidly, the biggest variety occurring in the Pacific, where the record – from Ecuador – is 220 lbs (100.24 kg).

Sailfish are pelagic and often hunt at current edges. Their broad diet includes shrimp, squids, herring, tuna and flying fish. Many methods are used to catch them, but the most common is trolling from an outrigger with filet, whole fish, plastic lures, feather jigs and spoons. When trolling with gray mullet, the speed should be around 5 knots – or fast enough for the bait to smash lightly on the surface. Baits are usually pulled 65-130 ft (20-40 m) behind the boat.

Like other billfish, this species tends to pop up behind or alongside a lure, and inspect it for a while before deciding either to strike or return to the depths. If the sailfish takes, it should be given ten seconds or so, in order to swim away with the bait before you make a strike.

Then the water surface explodes astern, and a silvery-purple monster catapults itself straight into the air. Its entire body shakes, then falls back in a cascade of spray. Usually it comes right up again, and this may go on for a dozen times, but at last it loses steam and the fight becomes more traditional.

A sailfish's dorsal fin is often extremely beautiful in the last stage of the fight. Stretched out, a yard high, it shifts in hue between purple and blue, with clear vertical rows of small black patches. These colors disappear immediately after the fish is dead.

Black marlin

The species *Makaira indica* occurs in tropical waters of the Indian and Pacific Oceans, but catches have also been reported from equatorial Atlantic waters. Among its favorite haunts are reefs and deep edges with nutritious upwelling water. Black marlin give a very powerful impression; they are identifiable, for instance, by their stiff pectoral fins, which cannot be folded in toward the body. They have slate-blue backs, but are silver-white under the lateral line.

Really big marlin are always females, and they can probably weigh over 2,200 lbs (1,000 kg), a metric ton. The record for rod-caught marlin is about 1,560 lbs (707 kg) and comes from Peru.

Black marlin are enormously popular sportfish and have made a big-game El Dorado of, for example, Cairn in Australia. There, as in other places, trolling with equipment in the heavyweight class is a quite common method. The fish takes artificial offshore lures as gladly as large, whole natural baits – bonito, flying fish, mackerel and squids – trolled at 3 to 6 knots. One should keep in mind that a black marlin wants to take some time before swallowing.

Blue marlin

As a rule, the species *Makaira nigricans* occurs between latitudes 45° N and 35° S in the Atlantic, and between 48° N and 48° S in the Pacific. It can also be found in the Indian Ocean.

The blue marlin has a cobalt-blue back, but silver-white sides and abdomen. Along its sides are light-blue vertical stripes, which disappear as soon as it dies. It feeds happily on small members of the mackerel family and on schools of squid. Thus it can normally be tempted with whole large baits such as bonito, gray mullet, mackerel, ballyhoo, runners and squid, although sometimes a small strip bait is enough. Natural baits are used chiefly along the east coast of the USA, while artificial lures predominate in Hawaii's world-famous marlin waters.

Striped marlin

The species *Tetrapturus audax* lives pelagically in the tropical and warm temperate expanses of the Indian and Pacific Oceans. It does not grow as large as the preceding kinds of marlin, but is reputed to be the most active on the hook.

Above: Nowadays it is increasingly common to release a billfish after the fight, thus giving other sportsmen the chance to write new fishing tales. This beautiful black marlin was caught off Pinas Bay (South Pacific, Panama) by Dr. Hans Pfenninger from Switzerland.
Left: Billfish in general are very handsome creatures, with a body shape that reveals their speed at swimming. They wander widely in the oceans, primarily through tropical and subtropical areas. But small swordfish visit Scandinavian waters almost every year.

Striped marlin have been called the "greyhounds" of the sea, due to their speed both under and on the surface. They weigh up to 550 lbs (250 kg) and the rod record, from New Zealand, is 493 lbs (224 kg). These fish are identified mainly by their upward-pointing dorsal fin, steel-blue back, and lavender-colored vertical stripes.

White marlin

Finally we have the species *Tetrapturus albidus* at latitudes 35-45° N in the Atlantic, as well as in the Gulf of Mexico, Caribbean and Mediterranean. It is lighter in color than any of the above marlin species, and the tip of its dorsal fin is rounded. Yet it, too, has beautiful blue vertical stripes along its sides.

White marlin are very popular among trollers with light equipment. They gobble most types of bait in coastal waters. The record rod-catch is 181 lbs (82.5 kg) from Brazil.

A boundless domain

The selection of fish species presented here is only a fraction of all those that exist in the world known as Pisces to scientists. Still, it includes the ones which are most appreciated, both on the fishing line and on the table. Some of them were doubtless what originally set the wave of sportfishing in motion around the Earth. And certainly they have pushed forward another wave with the enormous developments experienced by trolling in the past several years. It is worth remembering, once your rod is in hand or in the holder, not only that every fish species is unique – but also that each individual fish is. One should therefore be careful not to generalize extremely about their striking urges and fighting instincts. Match them on their own terms and discover that the world of fish is full of little giants!

Index